SECURE AND SURE

GRASPING THE PROMISES OF GOD

SECURE AND SURE

GRASPING THE PROMISES OF GOD

– ROBERT N. WILKIN –

Grace Evangelical Society

Irving, Texas

Cover and book design: Michael Makidon
Production: Cathy Beach and Michael Makidon

Library of Congress Cataloging-in-Publication Data
Wilkin, Robert N., 1952-
Secure and sure: grasping the promises of God / Robert N. Wilkin
Includes bibliographical references.
ISBN 0-9641392-7-8
1. Assurance. 2. Salvation. 3. Christian Life.

Requests for information should be addressed to:
Grace Evangelical Society
PO Box 155018
Irving, TX 75015-5018

Phone: 972.257.1160
Web: http://www.faithalone.org

This book is dedicated to the
Partners of Grace Evangelical Society
whose financial support, prayers,
and encouragement made
this book possible.
Additional thanks to
Zane Hodges,
Art Rorheim,
Steve Lewis,
Stan Nelson,
Cathy Beach,
Warren Wilke,
Mike Makidon,
Elliott Johnson,
George Meisinger,
Michelle Loupenay,
Mike and Letitia Lii,
my Mom, Jean Wilkin,
and my lovely wife, Sharon.

– TABLE OF CONTENTS –

Prologue 9
Introduction 11

A SURE FOUNDATION

1   Certainty: The Definition of Assurance 17
2   God's Word: The Source of Assurance 23
3   Biblical Promises: The Expressions of Assurance 29
4   Present Faith: The Basis of Assurance 37

A LIFE OF GREAT POTENTIAL

5   Walking in Assurance 45
6   The Greatest Source of Joy 53
7   The Power of Gratitude 57
8   See Less, Accomplish More 63
9   The Promise of Evangelism 71

OVERCOMING OBSTACLES

10   Will the Real Christian Please Stand Up? 81
11   Why Not Live Like the Devil? 93
12   Contemplating Approval 99
13   What if We Fail to Persevere? 107
14   Fractured Faith 113
15   Testing First John 121
16   Camouflage Christians 129
17   You Will Know Them by Their Fruits 137
18   Fact or Feeling? 149

ANSWERING OBJECTIONS

19   Why Is Certainty So Objectionable? 155
20   Only God Knows 161

21   Manageable Discomfort 169
22   Uncertainty Is Better than Any Other Option 181
23   A Myriad of Factors to Consider 193

Conclusion 201
Epilogue 205
Study Guide 207
Scripture Index 225
Subject Index 231
Annotated Bibliography 235
Testimonials 249

Prologue

Dark, alone, and uncertain—this was life for the frail five-year-old Phoenix twins. The news reports described their home as a roach-infested cage sealed in plastic, where they spent twenty hours of every day. While most children their age played tee-ball and video games, they remained caged like animals—unaware that there was another reality just outside their reach.

Oh, occasionally they enjoyed a respite from their prison when their mother allowed them to play outside for short periods. But those times were few and far between.

Night after night, day after day, they lay alone and uncertain. Who could they trust? Why were they being treated this way? Could they believe in anyone or anything? For them life held no certainty.

Such stories both horrify and incite us. We immediately identify with the plight of the two young children, unable to enjoy the freedom that should be theirs, forbidden the opportunity to grow and develop under the nurturing eyes of loving parents. We loathe the caregivers who abused them.

And yet, how many Christians choose to live a similar kind of existence? Many live as though God wants them to be fearful and uncertain of their eternal destiny.

Is this uncertainty necessary? The Bible answers with an emphatic *No!* Certainty that all who simply believe in Jesus are eternally secure can be found repeatedly in God's Word. And when it is, fear of hell vanishes and gratitude explodes within. And with gratitude comes a desire to share this wonderful news with others.

But what about you?

Have you picked up this book because you're unsure of your eternal standing with God and are searching for answers? Keep reading. I've been there and I share in this book the answers I've found over the course of thirty years of study on this key subject.

Or maybe you've received the gift of eternal life through faith in Christ, but you've lost the certainty you once had. Others have led you to believe that you need to look to your works to see if you measure up to what a "true Christian" should look like. When you look at your life, you feel it just doesn't measure up to what it should be. You doubt your security because your works are imperfect. This book was written for you as well. You can regain the certainty that you once had.

Possibly you have no doubts. You're certain you believe in Jesus and that you are secure forever. If so, this book explains Bible texts that are hard to understand and offers powerful motivations to stay sure and to share this message with others.

Secure and sure. That's what I hope for each of you.

Introduction

Some material possessions are pretty important: having a roof over your head, clothes to keep you warm in the winter, and a sufficient amount of food to eat and water to drink. These kinds of things are very important.

But the most important things in life are not things at all. For example, we all either long for or treasure the unconditional love and acceptance of our parents.

If you lacked the sure knowledge that your parents loved and accepted you, then your development as a child was hindered. Children who are not nurtured in an accepting home typically fail to maximize their early potential. In fact, many adults who have been living on their own for years find they still haven't gotten over the insecurity ingrained in them when they were children.

The same thing is true with your spouse. It's particularly important to know that your spouse loves and accepts you. It's vital to know that when you go home at night you will share fellowship with a person who loves and accepts you unconditionally.

But as important as all that is, it pales in significance to the most important possession any person can have in this life. Nothing is more valuable than the certain knowledge that you are irrevocably a member of God's family.

Do you know with certainty that you are eternally secure? Are you sure that you will spend eternity in the kingdom of God no matter what you might do or fail to do in the future? Is fear of hell a thing of the past for you?

If a Christian doesn't have this foundation, then he is greatly handicapped in his ability to please God and to serve Him. Assurance of salvation is the bedrock of a successful Christian life.

This book is directed toward those who are sure that they are eternally secure and toward those who are not. The former group will benefit by learning how to avoid losing assurance, how to answer objections, and how to disciple others on this key point. The latter group will profit by gaining the most important possession of all: certainty of their eternal destiny. Then once they gain that wonderful knowledge, they too can learn how to share this message with others.

Regardless of what type of church background you come from, you *can* be sure. You need not be condemned to a life of doubt and fear. Sadly, many people live as though Jesus didn't promise eternal life to the one who simply believes in Him. Many live as though He promised eternal life to those who serve Him faithfully over the course of their entire lives. That is not the good news of Jesus Christ. That is a man-made religion. It seems reasonable. But since it isn't what Jesus and the apostles taught, it isn't right.

This book is laid out to make it easy to follow. The first section deals with the basics of assurance: its definition, source, expressions, and basis.

The second section gives the practical benefits of being sure you are eternally secure: a vital platform for discipleship, daily joy and gratitude, the potential to believe in and strive for eternal rewards, and the ability to evangelize clearly.

There are many potential obstacles to assurance. Those obstacles are hurdled in the third section. In that section we consider the issue of false professors, motivations for obedience, the purpose of self-examination, perseverance, apostasy, First John, secret believers, fruit inspection, and the place of feelings in assurance.

The final section deals with objections leading pastors and theologians have to assurance as certainty. Evangelical leaders today present assurance as something that is less than certainty. We follow one pastor who says that only God knows who is truly regenerate. A Bible college professor and author is cited as suggesting that we must learn to live with discomfort about our eternal destiny. We look in on a leading theologian, author, educator, and head of a major ministry when he confesses his personal doubts about his eternal destiny and advises his readers that being uncomfortable with Jesus is the best we can hope for. Finally, a renowned pastor, seminary president, author, and national and international radio speaker is shown to eliminate the possibility of certainty by saying that one must consider a myriad of subjective factors before he can have "assurance." Each of these objections is countered with solid biblical evidence.

If you have searched for books on assurance, then you know that there are actually very few. However that isn't exactly the reason why I wrote on this subject.

I wrote on this subject because I haven't been able to find even one book on assurance that promotes the idea that a person can be certain he has eternal life. Admittedly, there are a few that speak of certainty in their titles or subtitles. But those books actually don't deliver what they promise.

For me this is not an academic issue, though I studied it intensely for seven years at Dallas Theological Seminary while getting my master's and doctor's degrees; and I've continued careful study on this subject in the twenty years since I completed my seminary studies.

For me this is a life-and-death issue. Certainty of eternal security is the promise of the gospel. Jesus promises the certain knowledge that all who simply believe in Him have everlasting life.

I gained certainty my senior year in college in 1972. That message gripped me and wouldn't let me go. For over three decades now I've devoted my life to sharing this message. If God gives me strength and length of years, and if the Lord tarries, I hope to keep on proclaiming this wonderful message for the next three or four decades as well.

If you are sure, you'll love the insights, encouragement, and ministry suggestions you'll find throughout this book.

If you aren't sure, you'll be challenged in this book to let go of that uncertainty. Why doubt God? Does that really make sense? Is it really better to go through life dangling over the pit of hell than to be certain you are eternally secure? Why not pray right now and ask God to reveal the truth to you? Don't blindly accept what I have to say. Examine the Scriptures to see if what I'm saying is true (Acts 17:11). It's God's Word that is sure. And that's why we can and should be sure! For God's Word is clear on this point: all who simply believe in Jesus Christ have eternal life. You can bank on it.

~ Section 1 ~

A SURE FOUNDATION

Most assuredly, I say to you,
he who believes in Me
has everlasting life.
John 6:47

— Chapter 1 —

CERTAINTY: THE DEFINITION
OF ASSURANCE

Life today, more than ever, is uncertain. Terrorist attacks that were only distant threats a few short years ago are now the subject of the daily news. The economic climate of the world is in constant flux and increasingly tenuous. Political regimes come and go with frightening regularity. Indeed nothing seems certain these days.

THE PREVALENCE OF UNCERTAINTY

Uncertainty permeates our Christian thinking as well. Many Christians are not sure where they are going when they die. Worse yet, they don't believe that possessing such certainty is possible.

When I came to faith in Christ in college, it was such a joy and relief to know that Jesus promised me *everlasting life* simply on the basis of believing in Him. Having believed that, I was absolutely sure I was eternally secure. Unfortunately, it didn't take long to find out that many who professed to be Christians disagreed with me. Many said we can't be sure we are eternally secure. And they tried to use the Scriptures to prove to me that we can't be sure!

But why is it, do you think, that God would want us to be in doubt about the most crucial issue of our lives—the certainty of our eternal standing? It's especially puzzling when you consider that the profound sense of gratitude certainty produces may be the single strongest motivator for the Christian to live for God. Obviously one can't be grateful for something about which he is uncertain.

BIBLICAL ASSURANCE IS CERTAINTY

The Bible is our source of truth and thus defines assurance for us. And what it says is clear. Believers can and should be certain that they have everlasting life. Works play no role in a person knowing he is eternally secure. The following verses present eternal life as the certain possession of all who simply believe in Jesus—an idea we will develop more fully in Chapter 2.

Let's first consider John 6:35. "And Jesus said to them, 'I am the bread of life. He who comes to Me shall never hunger, and he who believes in Me shall never thirst.'" After Jesus fed the 5,000 that day, the crowd came to Him saying, "Lord, give us this bread always" (John 6:34). They were hoping for the type of provision supplied to the Israelites for the forty years they wandered in the wilderness. But Jesus was referring to a miraculous type of bread and water. One who eats this bread or drinks this water will never hunger or thirst again!

"Coming to Jesus" is a metaphor for believing in Him. So, too, the symbolic drinking of living water and eating of the bread of life are figures of speech for believing in Him for eternal life. Note what Jesus promises to the one who believes in Him: that they will never hunger or thirst again. Clearly these are promises of eternal security to all who simply believe in Jesus.

Another passage that presents eternal life as the certain possession of all who simply believe in Jesus is John 11:25-27. It reads:

> Jesus said to her [Martha], "I am the resurrection and the life. He who believes in Me, though he may die, he shall live. And whoever lives and believes in Me shall never die. Do you believe this?" She said to Him, "Yes, Lord, I believe that You are the Christ, the Son of God, who is to come into the world."

Jesus makes two assertions about Himself in these great "I am" statements. He is the resurrection. And He is the life.

At the end of verse 25 Jesus explains the first declaration, "He who believes in Me, though he may die, yet he shall live." Most people think He is speaking of *spiritual life* in this verse. No. Jesus is "the resurrection" because He *physically raises* people from the dead! The promise here is that all who simply believe in Jesus are guaranteed to be raised from the dead and given glorified bodies. Clearly Jesus is speaking here of the resurrection of *believers*. Elsewhere in Scripture it is called *the first resurrection* (see Revelation 20:5). No believers will miss out on this resurrection. Jesus guarantees it.

The Lord explains His second assertion, "I am the life," in verse 26: "Whoever lives [physically] and believes in Me shall never die [spiritually]." That is a powerful promise, is it not? If true, then the one who merely believes in Jesus is *eternally* secure. Stop and think about it. What else could Jesus mean by "shall never die" other than such a person will never die spiritually? Never means never. If any believer in Jesus ever died spiritually, then Jesus lied. God's Word would not be true. All who simply believe in Jesus are eternally secure. This is the unavoidable conclusion of this verse. The only question that remains is "Do you believe this?"

Martha's response to that question was "Yes, Lord, I believe…" (John 11:27). Note that Martha does not hesitate to confess her faith in Jesus. She doesn't think it presumptuous. Martha was convinced that Jesus is the Christ, the Son of God who was prophesied to come into the world. And therefore, when He promised resurrection and eternal life to all who simply believe in Him, she knew He was telling the truth. She had no doubt about it.

I realize some people who read these verses will say, "But how do I know that I have *really* believed?"

What such a person needs to realize is that when he questions whether he has *really* believed, it's Jesus that he's doubting, not himself.

You see the issue is whether the Lord is trustworthy, not whether *we* are trustworthy. Here's a news flash. We aren't. Only God and His Word are completely and always worthy of our trust.

Martha was certain that she believed in Jesus and she affirmed that to Him. She didn't wonder if she *really* believed.

I'm passionate about assurance as certainty because that is what the Scriptures teach. But I must admit there's another reason for my passion. It's because I've seen the power of that certainty in my own life. It has produced and continues to produce love and gratitude in me toward God. In addition, it unlocks the Bible so that it fits together and makes sense. It should come as no surprise that when we believe what God says, especially something this important, that it has powerful repercussions in our lives.

— Chapter 2 —

GOD'S WORD: THE SOURCE OF ASSURANCE

In our postmodern culture, people who claim to be certain about anything are viewed with no small amount of skepticism. The only certainty today, it seems, is that you can't be certain! All but the most unreasonable, however, will acknowledge that at least some things in life are objectively certain.

For example, who doubts that two plus two equals four? That is objectively verifiable. So is citizenship. Just check your birth certificate or passport. Need to prove your voting status is active? Pull out your voter registration card. And if you want security clearance at work, just wear the photo ID badge you were issued when you were employed. None of these things are subjective or uncertain.

But what about the area of divine revelation? Can we be certain of things that God has recorded in His Word? In terms of the subject of this book, can we be specifically certain that we have *everlasting life?* And if we can, what is the source of that certainty?

People sometimes look to subjective factors in a misguided effort to determine their status in God's forever family. Many look to their works, but are haunted by the knowledge that the motives behind the good things they do are not always pure. Worse still, not all of their works are good. Some look to their love for other Christians, their commitment to Christ, and even whether or not they *feel* born again. Still others focus on how much they love God and hate sin only to find that sometimes their love for God is less than absolute and their hatred of sin wanes.

The only consistent thing that such introspection produces is doubt. It has no place in helping us know if we are citizens of heaven. Its purpose is to reveal to us the progress we are making in our walks with Christ (2 Corinthians 13:5). Our citizenship is unrelated to our performance.

CERTAINTY COMES FROM GOD'S WORD

To be certain, you need an objective standard. And there is one—the black and white promises of God to all who simply believe in Jesus. He assured, "He who believes in Me has everlasting life" (John 6:47). Do you believe in Jesus? If your answer is yes, then Jesus claims in this verse that you have everlasting life. Right?[1]

Now if you respond, "Well, I believe in Jesus, but I'm not sure whether or not I have everlasting life," then you clearly don't believe what Jesus said in John 6:47. If it is true, then it applies to everyone who believes in Jesus, even you.

There are scores of passages like this. For extensive evidence that the Word of God teaches eternal security for all who believe in Jesus, consider the following texts:

John 3:16. This may be the most famous verse in the Bible. Yet while it directly speaks to assurance, most don't apply it in that way. Jesus said, "For God so loved the world that He gave His only begotten Son, *that whoever believes in Him should not perish but have everlasting life*" (italics added). Those who believe in Jesus have eternal life and will never perish. That's the promise. If we believe the promise, we know we won't perish and we have everlasting life. It is that simple.

John 3:18. "He who believes in Him is not condemned." The one who believes in Jesus is in a state of non-condemnation. That is, he is a person who is justified, declared righteous before God. There is no such thing as a condemned believer. There never will be.

John 3:36. John the Baptist testified of Jesus, "He who believes in the Son has everlasting life." Did you note the verb tense? It is present tense. The believer *has* everlasting life. And since the life is everlasting, it can never cease. Works and feelings play no role in this—just faith.

Acts 15:7-11. The early church called a special council in Jerusalem to make an official decree on what Gentiles had to do to have eternal life. Paul, the apostle to the Gentiles, had been saying that all they had to do was believe in Jesus and they would be eternally secure. At the Jerusalem Council, as it has come to be called, Peter affirmed Paul's gospel, reminding the crowd that God sent him to Cornelius and his family so "that by my mouth the Gentiles should hear the word of the gospel and believe… purifying their hearts by faith…But we believe that through the grace of our Lord Jesus Christ we shall be saved in the same manner as they." The only condition is to believe the gospel. Hearts are purified by faith alone. Jews and Gentiles are saved in the same way, by faith alone in Jesus Christ alone. Peter is not expressing an opinion here. He is expressing fact. Peter is certain. And all who believe Peter's words are certain that they have everlasting life as well.

Acts 16:31. "Believe on the Lord Jesus Christ, and you will be saved" is Paul's answer to the Philippian jailer's question, "What must I do to be saved?" The one who believes this is sure that he is saved because God's Word is true and dependable.

Romans 4:5. "But to him who does not work but believes on Him who justifies the ungodly, his faith is accounted for righteousness." Justification—being declared righteous once and for all by God—occurs the moment one believes in Jesus. Works play absolutely no role in this. Did you notice those whom Paul says God justifies? *The ungodly!* We are all ungodly. Only by faith in Jesus can we be declared legally righteous in the sight of God. And all who believe this know that they are indeed justified, for that is what God promises. He promises certainty, not some possibility that is contingent on our future performance.

Galatians 3:6-7. "Abraham 'believed God, and it was accounted to him for righteousness.' Therefore know that only those who are of faith are sons of Abraham." Paul cites Genesis 15:6 concerning the justification of Abraham to validate his point that "a man is not justified by the works of the law but by faith in Jesus Christ" (Galatians 2:16). It is a fact that all who are "of faith," and only those people, are the spiritual descendants of the one whom Paul describes as "believing Abraham" (Galatians 3:9).

Ephesians 2:8-9. "For by grace you have been saved through faith, and that not of yourselves; it is the gift of God, not of works, lest anyone should boast." In this famous passage Paul reminds the Ephesian believers of the fact that they have been regenerated. Paul uses a perfect tense to make his point: *you have been saved.* That tense conveys a past event which continues forward. The Ephesian believers had been regenerated in the past ("[He] made us alive together with Christ," verse 5) and they will remain in that state forever. All believers are sealed eternally (Ephesians 1:13). There is no room for doubt here. Anyone who believes what Paul is saying knows that he has been made alive with Christ and that the life Jesus gave him is everlasting.

James 1:18. "Of His own will He brought us forth by the word of truth, that we might be a kind of firstfruits of His creatures." The half brother of Jesus reminds his readers, Jewish believers, that they were "brought forth" or born again "by the word of truth." Clearly James is referring to their *faith* in the truth of the gospel (compare James 1:3, "your faith"). This new birth is not dependent on some future action. It is an accomplished fact that occurs at the moment of faith in the word of truth.

1 Peter 1:22-23. "...Love one another fervently with a pure heart, having been born again, not of corruptible seed but incorruptible, through the word of God which lives and abides forever." Having called the readers to love one another with a pure heart, Peter explains *why* they are able to do that: because they have been born again. And the new birth, says Peter, comes from an incorruptible seed, the everlasting Word of God. Peter concludes with a citation from Isaiah 40, "The grass withers, and its flower falls away, but the word of the Lord endures forever" (1 Peter 1:24-25).

FIX YOUR EYES UPON JESUS

For some who are reading these words, the idea that we can be certain is difficult to grasp. Many have been steeped in the belief that it's impossible to be sure and that we must look to our works and our feelings to have some measure of confidence. But God's Word is clear on this. If you are willing to evaluate your tradition in light of the Bible, you can be sure.

Certainty comes from God's Word. Stand on His promises to the believer. Then you will be sure and you will also be grateful to God and highly motivated to live for Him.

---

[1] I realize that many people think that nearly everyone believes in Jesus. What they fail to understand is that biblical faith in Jesus is not faith that He existed, nor faith in His deity, nor even faith that He died for our sins and rose again. In the Bible, to believe in Jesus is to be convinced that He who died and rose again guarantees eternal life to all who simply believe in Him. This, most people definitely do not believe. In 1 Timothy 1:16 Paul spoke of himself as an example of all "who are going to believe in Him for everlasting life" (italics added). One is a believer when he is sure he has eternal life by faith in Jesus, apart from works.

— Chapter 3 —

BIBLICAL PROMISES: THE
EXPRESSIONS OF ASSURANCE

In a book on assurance it is important to mention an obvious yet widely unknown truth. It is this: *There is no special biblical word for assurance.*

If you take a concordance and look up all uses of the words *assure* and *assurance*, you will find that they never refer to assurance of one's relationship with God!

NO SPECIAL WORD

The fact that there's no special word for assurance shouldn't be that surprising. After all, there are many vital biblical doctrines for which there is no special word.[1]

For example, we have coined the word *Trinity* to refer to the fact that there is one God and yet three Persons—the Father, the Son, and the Holy Spirit. However, the term *Trinity* is not found anywhere in the Bible. God didn't choose to give us a word that expresses the idea of one God and yet three Persons.

The *Left Behind* series has caused a great deal of interest in the biblical doctrine known as the rapture. However, there is also no special word in the Bible for the catching up of living believers to meet Jesus in the air. Theologians coined the term *rapture*, from the Latin word which means *to be caught up*. But the word *rapture* does not occur in the English Bible.

The Bible teaches that Jesus is both fully God and fully man. Yet nowhere in the Bible do we find an expression that conveys that truth. Theologians have come up with a name for this too. They call the union of perfect humanity and full deity in the Person of Jesus *the hypostatic union*.

The same is true concerning what we call *assurance*. God didn't choose to give us a special name for it, so we don't have one.

STATEMENTS THAT CONVEY ASSURANCE

Assurance, the idea that all who believe in Jesus are certain that they are eternally secure, is the promise of the gospel. This promise is conveyed in many passages using a variety of words and phrases. Consider the following, most of which are drawn from the Gospel of John:

- "As many as receive Him, to them He gave the right to become children of God, to those who believe in His name" (John 1:12).

- "For God so loved the world that He gave His only begotten Son, that whoever believes in Him should not perish but have everlasting life" (John 3:16).

- "He who believes in Him is not condemned; but he who does not believe is condemned already..." (John 3:18).

- "He who believes in the Son has everlasting life; and he who does not believe the Son shall not see life, but the wrath of God abides on him" (John 3:36).

- "Whoever drinks of the water that I shall give him will never thirst. But the water that I shall give him will become in him a fountain of water springing up into everlasting life" (John 4:14).

- "Most assuredly, I say to you, he who hears My word and believes in Him who sent Me has everlasting life, and shall not come into judgment, but has passed from death into life" (John 5:24).

- "I am the bread of life. He who comes to Me shall never hunger, and he who believes in Me shall never thirst" (John 6:35).

- "He who believes in Me has everlasting life" (John 6:47).

- "I am the door. If anyone enters by Me, he will be saved, and will go in and out and find pasture" (John 10:9).

- "And I give them eternal life, and they shall never perish; neither shall anyone snatch them out of My hand" (John 10:28).

- "I am the resurrection and the life. He who believes in Me, though he may die [physically], he shall live [physically, that is, he will be resurrected by Jesus who is the resurrection]. And whoever lives [physically] and believes in Me shall never die [spiritually, since Jesus is the life]" (John 11:25-26).

- "And I know that His command is everlasting life. Therefore, whatever I speak, just as the Father has told Me, so I speak" (John 12:50).

- "He who is bathed needs only to wash his feet, but is completely clean; and you are clean, but not all of you" (John 13:10).

- "And truly Jesus did many other signs in the presence of His disciples, which are not written in this book; but these are written that you may believe that Jesus is the Christ, the Son of God, and that believing you may have life in His name" (John 20:30-31).

- "This is a faithful saying and worthy of all acceptance, that Christ Jesus came into the world to save sinners, of whom I am chief. However, for this reason I obtained mercy, that in me first Jesus Christ might show all longsuffering, as a pattern to those who are going *to believe on Him for everlasting life*" (1 Timothy 1:15-16, italics added).

- "And this is the promise that He has promised us—eternal life" (1 John 2:25).

While we could do the same with each passage listed, let's pick just one to show how these promises of eternal life are expressions of certainty. I've chosen a passage we briefly considered in the last chapter. Let's look more closely now.

In the passage cited from John 11, Jesus was talking to Martha four days after her brother Lazarus had died. There Jesus said that He promised the one who believes in Him two things: bodily resurrection and everlasting life.

As the resurrection He promises, "He who believes in Me, though He may die [physically], he shall live [physically]."

As the life He promises, "And whoever lives [physically] and believes in Me shall never die [spiritually]."

Then the Lord Jesus asked Martha a question that as far as we know He never asked anyone else. He asked Martha, "Do you believe this?" (John 11:26b).

Here was her chance to equivocate. She could talk about the moral commandments and perseverance and how she couldn't know if she really believed in Him until she died. That's the way many would answer today.

But she was definite. She was certain. She said, "Yes, Lord, I believe that You are the Christ, the Son of God, who is to come into the world" (John 11:27). Notice that the first word, "Yes," was a sufficient answer. But she went on to state *why* she was certain. She was convinced that Jesus guarantees bodily resurrection and no spiritual death for all who simply believe in Him because she was convinced that He is the Christ, the Messiah, the Son of God, who was promised in the Old Testament.

The only other use of the phrase "the Christ, the Son of God" in John's Gospel is found in his purpose statement for the book (John 20:31), cited above. This suggests that biblical faith in Jesus as "the Christ, the Son of God," is the conviction that anyone who simply believes in Him is eternally secure.

Clearly Martha believed the saving message and she knew it. She was certain. She was assured.

If you read on in John 11, you will see that Jesus does not rebuke her for stating that she believed Him. Clearly He is pleased by her profession. Of course, being omniscient, He already knew she believed in Him. But He wanted her to express her belief so that His statement and her response would be forever recorded as one of the greatest assurance statements in the Bible.

SIDE COMMENTS THAT CONVEY ASSURANCE

In addition to all of the direct assurance statements found in gospel promises, there are also many indirect assurance statements found in what we might call "side comments" to believers. By this I mean comments that help a believer understand a point that is indirectly related to assurance. Let's look at some of these and hopefully you'll see what I mean:

- "Nevertheless do not rejoice in this, that the spirits [demons] are subject to you, but rather rejoice because your names are written in heaven" (Luke 10:20).

- "Help these women who labored with me in the gospel, with Clement also, and the rest of my fellow workers, whose names are in the Book of Life" (Philippians 4:3).

- "Do you not know that your body is the temple of the Holy Spirit who is in you, whom you have from God, and you are not your own? For you were bought with a price; therefore glorify God in your body and in your spirit, which are God's" (1 Corinthians 6:19-20).

- "Of His own will He brought us forth [the new birth] by the word of truth, that we might be a kind of firstfruits of His creatures" (James 1:18).

- "And I, brethren, could not speak to you as to spiritual people but as to carnal, as to babes in Christ" (1 Corinthians 3:1).

- "For though by this time you ought to be teachers, you need someone to teach you again the first principles of the oracles of God; and you have come to need milk and not solid food" (Hebrews 5:12).

- "Even when we were dead in trespasses, [God] made us alive together with Christ (by grace you have been saved)...For by grace you have been saved through faith, and that not of yourselves; it is the gift of God, not of works, lest anyone should boast" (Ephesians 2:5, 8-9).

- "Can anyone forbid water, that these should not be baptized who have received the Holy Spirit just as we have?" (Acts 10:47).

Even those who don't believe that certainty is possible for believers prior to death must admit that there were people in the Bible who were absolutely certain. Clearly the disciples were sure, for Jesus directly told them that all of them except Judas were already clean. Paul indicated in inspired Scripture that the names of his co-workers, Euodia, Syntyche, and Clement were in the Book of Life (Philippians 4:3).

In the early 1990s, Dr. Ken Sarles and I were involved in a debate on faith and assurance. He indicated that we couldn't be absolutely certain we had eternal life, for we might not persevere. But when I pointed out that people like the apostles and Euodia, Syntyche, and Clement clearly were certain, he admitted that there were people in the Bible who indeed had been certain while they were alive.

Dr. Sarles had a unique answer as to why people in the time of Jesus could be sure, but we can't. He said the reason why some people in the early church were certain they had eternal life was because God specifically said so in the New Testament. He said that such certainty was not possible today since no one in this age is mentioned specifically by name in Scripture!

Frankly I still couldn't see how that answers the question. Why would God want the apostles, Paul's coworkers, and the believers in the churches to which the apostles wrote to be certain that they had eternal life, but no one today? If certainty was good for them, why wouldn't it also be good for us today?

Further, why can't we relate the promises of the gospel to our lives? And why can't we apply the side comments found in the Scriptures to our lives too?

We can be certain that Jesus is God, that the Bible is the Word of God, and so on. We can and should be certain, like Martha, that we believe in Jesus and that we have everlasting life.

YOU CAN BE SURE

Don't look for the word *assurance* in Scripture when you are trying to find verses that deal with what we call *assurance of salvation*. Instead, look for words, phrases, and statements like those I've given above that indicate that one who believes in Jesus has eternal life.

The Bible makes it clear that *what we believe Jesus for* is everlasting life (1 Timothy 1:16). Thus as long as we continue to believe in Him, we continue to be certain we have everlasting life.

Of course, as we will discuss fully in subsequent chapters, even if a believer loses his grip on the promise of everlasting life, he remains eternally secure. God never loses *His* grasp of anyone who comes to faith in Jesus (John 10:28-30).

---

[1] Another reason this shouldn't be surprising is because the English words *assure* and *assurance* are used in everyday speech to confirm all sorts of things. This is true theologically as well. For example, when I did a search of the word *assurance* in the Libronix Theological Library, I found that while there were hundreds of journal articles using that word, only rarely was assurance of eternal life being discussed. Consider what I found in three issues of the journal *Bibliotheca Sacra* (Volumes 142, 156, 157). I read of assurance that laws are not anti-Christian, that God judges evil men, that there will be a resurrection, that covenantal promises are true, that Jacob would prevail, that God will be victorious, that God providentially cares for His own, that God's grace is sufficient to see us through the hard times, that God hates sin, and so on.

— Chapter 4 —

PRESENT FAITH: THE BASIS OF ASSURANCE

Have you ever met someone who was looking to some past experience as the basis of their assurance? They prayed some prayer and put the date in their Bible. They walked an aisle after a particularly moving sermon. They made a commitment to Christ around a campfire—all meaningful experiences at the time to be sure. But there are some problems we encounter when we base our assurance on a past experience.

EXPERIENCE MAY BE INCONSISTENT WITH ETERNAL LIFE

The first difficulty we encounter when we base our assurance on a past experience is that assurance comes from God's Word, not from our experiences. Sadly, when asked about assurance, people point to all kinds of past experiences that have nothing to do with believing the good news.

No one would argue that prayer is an essential part of a believer's life. But more often than not when a person is urged to pray a prayer in response to an evangelistic tract or appeal, the focus of the prayer is on giving one's life to Christ, committing to serve Him, asking Him to take control of one's life, etc. Yet none of these things are conditions of eternal life.

It's interesting to note that there is not one account in Scripture where Jesus or His apostles ever told anyone to pray a prayer for everlasting life. Prayer is the way we as believers commune and fellowship with God. It is through this most intimate form of communication that we express our praise and thanksgiving to the Father, disclose our heaviest burdens, and make our deepest needs and requests known. But it is *faith* in Jesus, not *praying* to Him, that results in eternal life.

That brings us to walking an aisle. I think it's safe to assume that many people go forward at churches and evangelistic rallies without ever understanding and believing the saving truth of the gospel. Now admittedly some have come to faith when they came forward because a counselor clearly shared the saving message with them. But the act of going forward never in itself resulted in anyone's justification.

Similarly, the person who recalls committing his life to Christ is recalling a good thing, but something that carries no promise of eternal life. During my first year as a Bible college professor, I taught an evangelism course at Woodcrest College in East Texas. One of the assignments required the students to write their personal testimonies, making it crystal clear how they became Christians.

One young man submitted a confused testimony. He spoke of a time when he committed his life to Christ and came forward at a service, but never indicated in his paper that he had believed in Christ for eternal life. I returned the assignment and asked him to redo it and make it clear this time.

A few days later I received the revision. Though the wording in places had changed, the essential content was the same. He committed his life and walked an aisle. A bit frustrated, I called him into my office to discuss the matter.

"You've now written your testimony twice and you still haven't made it clear that when you were born again you came to believe that Jesus guarantees eternal life to all who simply believe in Him. Why are you having trouble doing that? Am I not being clear in the assignment?"

"No. The assignment is clear. I'm just telling you what happened when I got saved."

"What do you mean?"

"Well, it wasn't until this semester in your class that I learned that Jesus gives eternal life to all who simply believe in Him. Prior to this semester I thought we were saved by commitment and that if my commitment waned, then I would lose my salvation. So when you asked me to change my testimony, I was stuck because what I wrote in my paper is what really happened when I was saved many years ago."

"Now we're getting somewhere. So tell me, what does a person need to do to have eternal life?"

"The only condition is to believe in Him."

"Okay, when did you come to believe that?"

"A few weeks ago as you went over the gospel in class."

"Well, then," I asked, "when were you born again?"

"Wow. I get it now. I got saved this semester in your class!"

This young man's experience is not unique. I have counseled untold numbers of people who share a similar confusion. They had some experience years ago when they made a commitment and went forward. They perhaps drew closer to God. This is when they say they became a Christian. But then they go on to say that it wasn't until some later time when they came to be sure they had eternal life by faith in Jesus.

I try to help people see that regardless of what they felt when they had their experience, it wasn't until they believed in Christ for eternal life that they were born again. Even if it didn't seem special, the moment they knew for sure they had eternal life by faith in the Lord Jesus is the moment they entered God's forever family.

WE LIVE IN THE PRESENT

The second problem we encounter when we base our assurance on a past experience is that we don't live in the past. We live in the present. Since assurance is based on what I believe now, not on what I believed in the past, then if I am confused now, I lack assurance.

When I was teaching at Multnomah Bible College in Portland, the school newspaper ran a fascinating story of a recent graduate who had become a professing atheist. Upon leaving Multnomah, the young man had enrolled at a secular school. His studies in philosophy led him to reject his former beliefs, even to the point that he ceased believing in the existence of God.

The interviewer asked him if during his time at Multnomah he had believed the fundamentals of the faith. Had he believed that Jesus is the Son of God? That Jesus died on the cross for his sins and rose bodily from the dead? That because of his faith in Jesus he had eternal life? This atheist assured the interviewer that he had formerly believed all these things. But now, he said, he realized all those things were on par with Greek mythology.

We can have assurance now only if we believe the promise of God now. Even if we believed His promise in the past, if we no longer believe it, then we aren't sure we are saved because the only way to have assurance is to believe the promise now.

Of course, loss of certainty doesn't mean loss of eternal life. Eternal life is eternal. Once we believe in Jesus for eternal life, we are secure *forever,* even if we later lose assurance.

REJOICE THAT YOU ARE SURE TODAY

I don't know the exact day I was born again. You may wonder why. The answer is simple. I invited Jesus into my heart during high school, but continued to lack assurance that I was going to heaven when I died. During college I related this to an Athletes in Action staff member, Warren Wilke, and asked him to help me gain assurance.

Warren thought I was a confused believer. In reality, I was a confused *unbeliever* because I had never believed in justification by faith alone.

Like the student in my earlier illustration, I didn't realize that it was at the moment when I believed in Jesus for eternal life as Warren was explaining the Scriptures to me, that I became a Christian.

I knew it was at that time I became convinced that Jesus guarantees eternal life to all who believe in Him. I just didn't realize that was the day I was born again. In other words, I didn't understand that believing in Jesus is not only the condition of assurance, but also of eternal salvation.

As a result, I can't tell you what day or week or even month I was born again. I know it was in the Fall of 1972.

Here's a very valuable piece of advice for all who, like me, can't remember precisely when they first came to believe in Christ for eternal life. *Give up trying to figure out when you were born again. Simply rejoice that you are sure today that you are eternally secure by virtue of your faith in Christ.*

Assurance is based not on what you did or even believed in time past. It's based on what you believe right now. So look to Jesus and His promise of eternal life to all who simply believe in Him and you will remain sure you have eternal life. It's that simple.

~ Section 2 ~

A LIFE OF GREAT POTENTIAL

*I have come that they may
have life, and that they may
have it more abundantly.*
John 10:10b

— Chapter 5 —

WALKING IN ASSURANCE

Is it possible to be a disciple of Jesus Christ and yet not be sure you have eternal life? Well, since a disciple by definition is a learner, the answer is a qualified yes. A person can be learning about Jesus and not yet be sure he has eternal life.

But a person can't be a *mature* disciple unless he's sure he has eternal life. For you see, doubts about one's relationship with God will never produce consistent growth or Christian maturity. Only certainty can do that.

Let's look at some key discipleship truths that cannot be properly understood or applied until one is sure he has everlasting life.

KEY DISCIPLESHIP TRUTHS AND ASSURANCE

Many crucial discipleship principles can only be grasped by those with certainty. Three of these are: 1) Gratitude that motivates us to persevere in our Christian walks; 2) Proper application

of Scriptures dealing with chastisement and eternal rewards; and
3) Liberty from legalism that entraps the unsure.

Grateful for Certainty

Paul said, "The love of Christ constrains us" (2 Corinthians
5:14). While the love of Christ motivated Paul, it didn't motivate
me. That is, it didn't until I knew I had eternal life. As long as I
feared hell and looked to my faulty works, I couldn't experience
the love of Jesus.[1]

Anyone who lacks certainty obviously doesn't know if he is
eternally secure. Such a person doesn't know if he is in God's
family now or if he will be in His family forever.

Like the person with a lottery ticket before the drawing takes
place, a person who lacks assurance can't be grateful for something
that he may well never obtain. Unless there is some objective way
of knowing that you have eternal life, gratitude is beyond your
reach.

Correct Application

The Scriptures used to be a quagmire of contradictions for me.
In some places they spoke of God's mercy and love and grace. I'd
read that whoever believes in Jesus has everlasting life. But many
other passages warned that only those who endure to the end shall
be saved, that the soul that sins shall die, that it's a terrifying thing
to fall into the hands of the living God, and so on.

Since application is based on interpretation, if you misinter-
pret you also misapply. I was convinced that every warning in the
Bible concerned hell, without regard for the possibility that these
warnings could be referring to negative consequences in this life or
at the Judgment Seat of Christ.

On the other hand, I believed that every passage that spoke of blessing based on faithfulness concerned heaven, because I had no concept of the doctrines of temporal or eternal rewards. So those passages that deal with rewards also increased my despair since I misunderstood what they meant.

But what I later came to realize is that when we fall into a legalistic mindset, we are spiritually defeated (Romans 7:13-25). The key to applying those texts is to focus on Jesus and pleasing Him and hearing His "Well done, good servant" (Luke 19:17). But at that point I couldn't do that because I didn't yet understand or believe in justification by faith alone.

Only the Truth Can Set Us Free

The Lord Jesus told a group of people who had just come to faith in Him, "If you abide in My word, you are My disciples indeed. And you shall know the truth, and the truth shall set you free" (John 8:31-32). Jesus clearly says that it is the truth, not error, which sets us free from bondage to sin.

A legalist is someone who seeks to gain confidence that he will make it into the kingdom by focusing on God's commands and his own works (Luke 18:9-14). Yet legalism doesn't produce true righteousness and it doesn't produce assurance. The legalist is greatly handicapped in his ability to please God, even if he's born again.[2]

A group of people we now call *Judaizers* attacked the churches of Galatia that Paul had planted. The Book of Galatians is Paul's defense of the gospel and his attack on legalism. There Paul says that legalism produces hatred, not love: "But if you bite and devour one another, beware lest you are consumed by one another" (Galatians 5:15). This he sets in contrast with what is produced by the love that comes from true Christian liberty: "For you, brethren, have been called to liberty; only do not use liberty as an opportunity for the flesh, but through love serve one another" (Galatians 5:13). Paul concludes this section by saying, "Let us not become conceited, provoking one another, envying one another" (Galatians 5:26).

No matter how well intentioned, legalism hinders rather than aids discipleship.

GOD ISN'T A TOXIC PARENT

Assurance isn't simply a comforting doctrine. It's foundational to discipleship. If we want to live a life that is pleasing to God, we must be sure we are His children and will remain so forever.

To deny the power of assurance in discipleship would be akin to denying the power of assurance of parental love for a child's growth and maturity. Remember the five-year-old Phoenix twins I told you about in the Prologue? After being treated like animals by their parents, they were greatly handicapped in their ability to grow and mature properly.

It's imperative for a child to know that his parents love him unconditionally in order to develop into a mature and healthy adult.

In her bestselling book *Toxic Parents: Overcoming Their Hurtful Legacy and Reclaiming Your Life*, Dr. Susan Forward tells a powerful story of a 48-year-old dentist, whom she calls *Phil*. He came to her because of his extreme shyness, feelings of inadequacy, and hypersensitivity. When she asked about his childhood, Phil fell silent. With some coaxing, Dr. Forward found out that the origin of his feelings of worthlessness came from teasing at the hands of his father. The following story broke my heart. It perfectly illustrates the problem many have in their view of God.

Phil spoke about a time when he was six and his dad led him to believe he might not really be a member of the family at all:

> It was bad enough being teased, but sometimes
> he'd really scare me when he'd say things like:
> "This boy can't be a son of ours, look at that face.
> I'll bet they switched babies on us at the hospital.
> Why don't we take him back and swap him for the
> right one." I was only six, and I really thought I
> was going to be dropped off at the hospital.[3]

Dr. Forward explained that "Phil, like any young child couldn't distinguish the truth from a joke, a threat from a tease."[4]

Some church people are like that. They are unable to distinguish truth from error concerning the promise of eternal life. Many become confused when well-meaning pastors warn them that they may not be children of God.

Concerning assurance, one pastor writes:

> If a person fails to love and obey the Lord through
> the trials of life, then there is no evidence that he
> or she is a true believer. How many people do you
> know who followed Christ for a while, had some
> trouble in their lives, and then went away from
> Him? (cf. John 6:66) Although they may have
> made a profession of faith in Christ, they cannot
> be identified as those who love Him because
> their lives are not characterized by an enduring
> obedience.[5]

Two pages later he made this clarification:

> Now I want you to keep in mind an important
> distinction. Endurance does not earn eternal life,

but it is the proof of true faith and love, and that is rewarded by eternal life.[6]

As long as endurance in obedience is required to prove one is truly a child of God, we're all like 6-year-old Phil. If endurance is "rewarded by eternal life [!],"[7] then until we have endured to the end, we will wonder if we are truly in God's family at all.

Phil's dad may have been well-meaning. But he was in some sense a toxic parent. God is not like Phil's dad. God isn't a toxic parent. Just the opposite. He wants His children to remain sure from the moment they come to faith until they leave this earth. Security promotes Christlikeness. Insecurity does not.

It's imperative for the believer to know that he's unconditionally a member of God's family. Only with such knowledge is he able to grow and mature into the image of Jesus Christ.

---

[1] Admittedly, a person might be grateful that Jesus died for him even if he wasn't sure he had eternal life. However, fear of hell is so powerful that it either eliminates gratitude for Jesus' death (as it did in my case) or else it greatly minimizes it. Paul's gratitude for Jesus' death on his behalf was clearly based on his assurance of eternal life.

[2] A person who is born-again can be legalistic in two ways. First, through incorrect teaching he may become confused on the gospel and lose his assurance. Thus he tries to be justified by works (Galatians 5:4). Second, a regenerate person can be legalistic in the area of sanctification. He does this by fixing his eyes on the commandments (sometimes man-made), rather than on Jesus (Romans 7:13-25).

[3] Susan Forward, *Toxic Parents: Overcoming Their Hurtful Legacy and Reclaiming Your Life* (New York: Bantam Books, 1989), p. 98.

[4] Ibid.

[5] John F. MacArthur, Jr., *Saved without a Doubt: How to Be Sure of Your Salvation* (Wheaton: Victor Books, 1992), p. 151.

[6] Ibid., p. 153.

[7] That would mean that eternal life is *not* a gift, for in Romans 4:4 Paul uses the Greek word for *reward* when he says, "Now to him who works, the wages [rewards] are not counted as grace but as debt." Yet Paul continues, "But to him who does not work but believes on Him who justifies the ungodly, his faith is accounted for righteousness."

— Chapter 6 —

THE GREATEST SOURCE OF JOY
Luke 10:20

Have you ever been really happy about something only to discover that you were happy about the wrong thing? I have.

Rushing through college, I graduated in three years. That made me happy because I had accomplished my goal of getting my bachelor's degree and getting it quickly. But something else should have been my main source of joy.

Learning how to think and analyze should have been much more precious to me. The degree was secondary. The classes I took to get my biology degree taught me how to think. That helped me greatly when I later went to seminary. It has helped me ever since.

I should have been most joyful over how I'd changed. The new me that emerged after college was what was really important about my university days. That is especially true since I was born again during my senior year.

We always should take more joy over our *being* than over our *doing*.

I recently watched a documentary about former heavyweight boxing champion George Foreman. It was fascinating.

After Foreman beat Joe Frazier and became the heavyweight champion, he was overjoyed at reaching his lifelong goal. He lost sight of who he was and what he was becoming. He was caught up in what he had done.

His fame brought many women in his path and he became unfaithful to his wife. He had three children by three different women, all out of wedlock, in a one-year period.

Later he lamented what he had become during those years. He was no longer impressed by his fame or fortune. Now who he really was inside became his greatest source of joy.

Luke 10 recounts a time when Jesus commissioned seventy of His disciples to carry the message of the kingdom from city to city. While ministering, they encountered people who were demon possessed. Since Jesus had given them authority to cast out demons, they did so.

They returned ecstatic, saying that "even the demons are subject to us in Your name" (verse 17). Understandably, the disciples felt like they were on top of the world with this new found authority.

The problem was, they were focusing on the wrong thing. While it's great to do important things in service of the Lord Jesus, our *greatest* source of joy should always be that we are eternally secure members of His kingdom.

Think back to a time when you achieved something that was really awesome. How did you feel? Wasn't it great? But are our best accomplishments really the most important things about us?

Jesus replied to the disciples, "Nevertheless, do not rejoice in this, that the spirits are subject to you, but rather rejoice because your names are written in heaven" (verse 20).

There's a lesson here for all of us. We should find our greatest source of rejoicing not in what God allows us to do in His name, but in the fact that our names are written in heaven. The latter concerns our *being*, not our *doing*. That we are born-again people is awesome. Nothing we can do in service for Christ can overshadow the wonder of eternal security.

There's no greater source of joy in life than knowing you're eternally secure. My hope for those of you who lack assurance is that this book will help you find the joy that surpasses all others. If you have assurance, my desire is for you to find your greatest joy in it, thank God for it, and share it with everyone you can.

I believe the Lord was telling the seventy, and ultimately believers of all ages, that the ministry we do for God should spring from a joyful heart. While there is nothing wrong with being happy about our accomplishments, the accomplishments mean next to nothing if we are on our way to a Christless eternity. Accomplishments have eternal significance only if we know ourselves to be eternally secure.

What better source of joy is available than the knowledge that our names are written in the Book of Life?

In addition, we need to remember that our accomplishments may not always be grand. Sometimes we muddle along in life seemingly accomplishing very little. At those times it is even more important that we rejoice in our eternal security.

I've heard stories of missionaries who have worked for years on a field and not led even one person to faith in Christ. If their joy were dependent on their accomplishments, they would be consigned to a ministry of misery even though they might well have been serving God faithfully.

If you have believed in the Lord Jesus for eternal life, then you have eternal life and your name is written in heaven. Put that in four-inch headlines. Being a man or woman or boy or girl whose name is written in heaven is a big deal. Rejoice in that!

— Chapter 7 —

THE POWER OF GRATITUDE

In the last chapter we saw that the Lord Jesus wishes us to find our greatest source of joy in our eternal security. In this chapter we will discuss the power such joy can exert in our everyday lives.

Have you ever been extremely grateful for something that someone did for you? A pastor friend of mine, Woody Woodward, was so grateful for all his father had done for him over the years that he gave him one of his kidneys!

My first grade teacher, Mrs. Lamb, was wonderful to me. She made me feel special, loved, and cared for. I was a hyperactive child, but that year I somehow interrupted and squirmed less than I ever did before or after. I worked so hard in class to please her. Gratitude led me to do my best for her.

How do you feel when some stranger smiles and waves at you? Don't you experience a little burst of joy? And I bet you smile and wave right back.

How about when someone lets you into a line of traffic? Don't you wave your appreciation?

In all things, whether little or big, you know that when someone has shown you kindness, you want to do something for him. It's not that you *have to* repay his kindness. You just *want to* do so.

It stands to reason, then, that Christians, of all people, should be the most grateful, especially to God who has given us the greatest gifts anyone could ever give (life, health, giftedness, opportunities, eternal life, and the indwelling ministry of the Holy Spirit).

Let's begin by thinking about the relationship between assurance and gratitude.

UNFOUNDED ASSURANCE PHOBIAS

One of the main arguments I hear against eternal security is that if the doctrine were true then all the boundaries of civil behavior would be down. Believers would be motivated to live in some uncontrolled way and possibly even do horrible things just because they could.

Does this fear make sense to you? Well, it did to me for about fourteen years. I was one of those who feared eternal security for I had been taught that it led to ungodliness.

I was terribly afraid of hell during this time and had little hope of avoiding it. I certainly didn't feel grateful for eternal security. The reason was simple. I didn't believe in it.

The funny thing was that once I saw this doctrine clearly taught in the Bible, my phobia about licentiousness vanished. Where I had been afraid that believing in eternal security would move me to do drugs or be involved in immorality, I found instead that I was moved to confess my holier-than-thou attitude, to tell others about the grace of God, and to live a godlier life than before. Legalism really hadn't worked for me.

Eternal security produced a profound sense of gratitude in my life. Never before had I experienced a genuine concern for others. Prior to being certain I was eternally secure, I was outwardly religious to the point that people were repelled by me and my pharisaical attitudes. After I gained certainty, people began to see the changes in me and view me as someone who cared about them. I had quit being a phony. People could now identify with me. I had come to see that I was a sinner just like everyone else. I no longer felt I had to be, or could be, better than others to make it into the kingdom. People picked up on this attitude right away.

I began to share my newfound faith with friends and strangers as well, longing for them to experience the joy that certainty of eternal life brings.

THE UNDERRATED MOTIVATOR

I believe the reason gratitude is underrated as a motivator in Christianity is that so many traditions deny the possibility of certainty prior to death. If you can't be certain, you can't be grateful for having eternal life. Therefore, in that way of thinking, gratitude about one's eternal destiny must not be important.

Among the people I know that are certain, gratitude is viewed as priceless. This is especially true of those of us who struggled for years with fears about our eternal destiny due to legalistic religious influences. Once those bound by fear are set free, there's such a surge of powerful gratitude that it makes dishonoring God unconscionable.

Assurance has the power to revolutionize your service for Christ. People without certainty are rightfully reluctant to share their faith. What good news do they have to share with others? After all, they aren't sure where they're going when they die so they live each day in fear of hell. The best they can do is "help" others be unsure where they're going as well! Only those who are certain have a powerful motivation to tell others what they've discovered.

WHAT GRATITUDE DID FOR THE APOSTLE PAUL

Probably few people in all of history have ever been more legalistic than Saul of Tarsus. He was an expert in the Law of Moses. When Christianity began to spread, Saul became its leading persecutor.

But the risen Lord Jesus changed Saul. While on his way to Damascus to arrest Christians, Saul was confronted face to face by Jesus Christ Himself. Saul came to faith as a result of the direct witness of the risen Messiah.

The change in Saul was so dramatic that Christians at first thought he was only pretending to believe in Jesus. Imagine this archenemy suddenly preaching Jesus.

In Second Corinthians Chapter 11 Paul defended his apostolic ministry. People were telling the believers in Corinth that Paul wasn't really God's spokesman. They were attempting to undermine his ministry.

Paul's defense is a remarkable testimony to the power of gratitude:

> Are they Hebrews? So am I. Are they Israelites? So
> am I. Are they ministers of Christ?—I speak as a

fool—I am more: in labors more abundant, in stripes above measure, in prisons more frequently, in deaths often. From the Jews five times I received forty stripes minus one. Three times I was beaten with rods; once I was stoned; three times I was shipwrecked; a night and a day I have been in the deep; in journeys often, in perils of waters, in perils of robbers, in perils of my own countrymen, in perils of the Gentiles, in perils in the city, in perils in the wilderness, in perils in the sea, in perils among false brethren; in weariness and toil, in sleeplessness often, in hunger and thirst, in fastings often, in cold and nakedness—besides the other things, what comes upon me daily: my deep concern for all the churches.

—2 Corinthians 11:22-28

Legalism didn't make him such a man. It was the grace of God which produced a powerful sense of gratitude in Paul. That gratitude led him to maximize his life for Christ in the face of tremendous opposition.

WE LOVE HIM BECAUSE
HE FIRST LOVED US

Do you love Jesus? If not, you need spiritual defibrillation. It's time to attach the gratitude paddles and get shocked out of your spiritual lethargy.

John said, "We love Him because He first loved us" (1 John 4:19). Paul said, "The love of Christ compels us, because we judge thus: that if One died for all, then all died; and He died for all, that those who live should live no longer for themselves, but for Him who died for them and rose again" (2 Corinthians 5:14-15).

If you are certain you are eternally secure by faith in Jesus, then you have grounds for great love for the Lord Jesus. Gratitude is the natural response to such love. But if you aren't certain, then you need to settle that issue first so that you can experience the power of gratitude and really live.

— Chapter 8 —

SEE LESS, ACCOMPLISH MORE

Walking through airports on speaking trips, I regularly see a huge advertisement that pictures Tiger Woods straining to read a putt. In the background is a huge crowd ringing the green. Tiger has his hands cupped around the side of his head, touching his cap. His field of vision has been reduced so that he only sees straight ahead: the line of the putt.

Normally I just glance at the tag line. But recently I stopped to read it. "Sometimes you have to see less to accomplish more." It hit me as I thought about it that that is essentially what the Lord says about the doctrine of eternal rewards. In order to set our heart, our vision so to speak, on heavenly treasure, we must take our eyes off of earthly treasure (Matthew 6:19-21). We have to see less of this world in order to accomplish more for the next world.

Undue focus on material wealth or possessions takes our attention off of eternal rewards. There is, however, a less obvious distraction than worldly treasures. It's a spiritual concern: fear of hell.

Fear of hell doesn't reduce our ability to think about rewards; it eliminates it. Contrary to popular thinking, fear of hell is not a good thing for Christians.

We've already established that knowing for sure that you're eternally secure and that you won't go to hell, in and of itself should produce gratitude which is a powerful motivator for living the Christian life. However, combining gratitude with a desire to please God and earn eternal rewards produces a heightened longing for eternal significance and increased opportunity to serve the King.

Assurance is totally compatible with the doctrine of eternal rewards. Anyone who is sure he has eternal life is a great candidate to believe in eternal rewards. The Bible has lots of verses that teach that after this life is over, believers will be judged according to their works. The only way to harmonize that truth with the guarantee of eternal life to all who merely believe in Jesus—apart from works, is to recognize that the Lord Jesus will be giving believers rewards after this life is over.

This compatibility even works the other way around. If a person comes to believe in the doctrine of eternal rewards, he's a great candidate to believe in eternal security.

Now I must admit I have heard preachers who espouse Lordship Salvation—the view that only those who submit to Christ's Lordship and persevere in that commitment will escape eternal condemnation—occasionally mention the doctrine of rewards. Yet I find they do so rarely and without much emphasis, for in their system only those who persevere in faith and good works make it into the kingdom. Hopefully at some point their eyes will be opened to the fact that since all who persevere are rewarded, perseverance is a requirement of reward, not kingdom entrance.

I believe that an understanding of the doctrine of rewards is a means by which Lordship Salvation people can be set free.

My friend Tom is a case in point. A five-point Calvinist and mild Lordship Salvationist, Tom was quite familiar with the doctrine of eternal rewards, but he just wasn't convinced. Then one day he was preparing a sermon on 2 Peter 1:5-11. That day he came face to face with Peter's appeal to *add to your faith* certain character qualities so that a rich entrance to the kingdom *will be added* to you. Tom saw that the same Greek verb (*epichoregeō*) appears in verses 5 and 11. He became convinced that it took more than faith (you must *add to your faith*), in order to get this rich entrance to the kingdom.

Suddenly the dominoes began to fall. As his understanding of this passage changed, so did his understanding of hundreds of others. Almost instantly Tom came to believe in the grace of God, in eternal rewards, and in certainty.

INSECURITY AND A DESIRE FOR REWARDS?

Though it's hypothetically possible for a person to be motivated by the prospect of eternal rewards and yet not be certain he has everlasting life, there are two reasons why it rarely, if ever, happens.

The first reason is that a person who fears hell is so concerned about just getting into the kingdom he has no energy left to consider possible rewards once he's there. To him, getting into the kingdom *is* the reward.

The second reason is that the person who lacks certainty interprets eternal rewards passages as dealing with kingdom entrance.

Let's briefly look at a few rewards passages which are often misunderstood as teaching that one must persevere in order to *enter* the kingdom.

MISINTERPRETING REWARDS PASSAGES

1 Corinthians 9:24-27

In this famous passage Paul indicates that believers are striving for a "prize," which he calls "an imperishable crown" (verses 24-25). What does Paul mean in verse 27 when he concludes, "But I discipline my body and bring it into subjection, lest, when I have preached to others, I myself should become disqualified"?

A few years ago in Miami a seminary professor who also pastors a large church told me that Paul was indicating in this passage he wasn't sure he was born again! In other words Paul was saying that he was afraid if he didn't persevere, he would go to hell. To make matters worse, the professor/pastor went on to say that he himself wasn't sure he was born again and that no one could be until they died.

Talk about misunderstanding a passage! Paul's point is that having Christ's *approval* requires perseverance. The word translated *disqualified* actually means *disapproved*. Paul feared disapproval, not hell. Elsewhere Paul uses the same word without the negative prefix[1] to call Timothy to strive to be an *approved* workman who need not be ashamed (2 Timothy 2:15).

Second Timothy 2:12

Paul says, "If we endure, we shall also reign with Him." Many understand Paul to be saying that those who endure in their confession and obedience *will get into the kingdom*, but those who do not, that is, those who deny Christ, will be denied kingdom entrance by Him. They believe that all who enter the kingdom will rule with Christ. Thus failure to rule is failure to enter.

Yet this is a complete reversal of what Paul is saying in verse 11: "If we have died with Him we shall also live with Him." Paul said elsewhere "I have been crucified with Christ; it is no longer I who lives but Christ lives in me; and the life which I now live in the flesh I live by faith in the Son of God" (Galatians 2:20). By extension *every person* who places his faith in Christ for eternal life has died (positionally) with Christ. Paul says here that all who have died with Him, that is, all who believe in Him, shall also live with Him.

In verse 13 Paul carries it further: "If we are faithless, He remains faithful; He cannot deny Himself." Since Jesus promised that "He who believes in Me has everlasting life," then that is true even if we fail to endure. Jesus can't deny Himself and that is what failing to keep His promise would be.

Ruling with Christ is a reward for work well done, not something all believers are guaranteed in the kingdom. When we fail to see this, we turn this passage—which is intended to motivate us to live in light of the possibility of ruling with Christ—into one that destroys any possibility of assurance prior to death.

James 5:9

"Behold, the Judge is standing at the door!" For many this is a warning that if we lose sight of Jesus' soon return and live in an unloving way, we will miss getting into the kingdom. Yet James is referring to the fact that every believer will be judged at the Judgment Seat of Christ (the Bema) and we should live in light of that fact. The issue is not whether we are born again. The issue is how we will fare at the Bema.

1 John 2:28

"And now, little children, abide in Him, that when He appears, we may have confidence and not be ashamed before Him at His coming." Many see in this passage a warning about hell! They believe that being ashamed before Christ at His second coming means that one is not a "true" believer and that he will be cast into the lake of fire.

Yet this is the theme verse of John's first epistle and it is addressed to "little children." Unbelievers are not the spiritual children of an apostle! Indeed not only are they his spiritual children, but John loves them greatly as evidenced by the term of endearment, *little children.*

The body of First John ends with another charge regarding the Bema (see 1 John 4:17-19). There is a "day of judgment" ahead for every child of God (1 John 4:17). John is referring to the Judgment Seat of Christ, the Bema (compare 2 Corinthians 5:9-10). Only if God's love is perfected or matured in our lives will we have confidence at the Bema.

To take 1 John 2:28 and 4:17-19 as justification verses turns the Christian life into a competition to see if we can be good enough to merit kingdom entrance. Sadly, not only does that fail to produce assurance, but it means the person doesn't even believe the good news that Jesus guarantees eternal life to all who simply believe in Him.

WE CAN ACCOMPLISH MORE

Examples could be multiplied, but the point is clear. Many people are distracted by fear of hell. They find it practically impossible to see any passages as dealing with eternal rewards because their fear of hell confuses them. They do not believe that all who simply believe in Jesus are eternally secure (e.g., John 11:26). They believe that eternal security is tied to perseverance in good works. Thus perseverance can't be a condition of special rewards since all who make it into the kingdom persevere in good works.

Admittedly fear of hell causes many other distractions besides keeping a person from focusing on laying up treasure in heaven. Fear of hell can so paralyze a person that they are afraid of doing *anything* for fear that they will do something that will cause them to go to hell. However, in this chapter we've focused on how fear of hell distracts a person from focusing on eternal rewards. And that in itself is a major drawback, for the Lord Jesus commanded us to set our hearts on treasure in heaven (Matthew 6:19-21).

Yet until one is sure he has eternal life by faith in Jesus, he *cannot* have such a mindset. Once someone knows he has eternal life, the distraction of insecurity is blocked out, and then he will have the ability, as the Tiger ad illustrates, to accomplish more!

---

[1] The Greek word translated *disqualified* in 1 Corinthians 9:27 is *adokimos*. The letter "a" is a prefix that negates the meaning of *dokimos*, which means *approved* (e.g., 2 Timothy 2:15). We do the same thing in English. One who believes in God is called a theist. One who does not is called an atheist.

— Chapter 9 —

THE PROMISE OF EVANGELISM

In the New Testament assurance isn't a separate issue from the gospel because it is inherently contained in the gospel promises themselves. Assurance is an essential element in evangelism.

EVANGELIZE FIRST, ASSURE LATER

Nevertheless, it has become common in Christianity to separate the two. People use a two-step approach. First they evangelize. They attempt to "lead a person to Christ." Second—and only if the listener responds positively—they do "follow-up" which begins and centers on assurance.

That's a tragic separation of two things that cannot be separated. *You can't lead a person to Christ without telling them what it is that they must believe about Him in order to have eternal life.* The promise Jesus makes to the one who believes in Him is *everlasting life*. Thus until a person understands that, they have not yet understood the good news.

Let me illustrate this from John 6:47. I'll give a hypothetical conversation between me and a person named Steve.

"Steve, in John 6:47 Jesus said, 'He who believes in Me has everlasting life.' Do you believe in Jesus?"

"Yes, I believe in Jesus."

"Well then, Steve, according to this promise, what do you have?"

"Well, Bob, if we just took this verse in isolation it would seem that just by believing in Jesus I have everlasting life."

"Right."

"But we know from other verses that you must keep the moral commandments to make it to heaven. So it isn't as simple as just intellectually believing in Jesus."

"So what are you saying, Steve? Is Jesus wrong when He says that 'He who believes in Me has everlasting life'?"

"No, of course not. What I'm saying is that we must take the whole counsel of the Bible into account. You can't just pick out a few verses here and there."

"Well, Steve, Scripture never contradicts itself. What Jesus said in John 6:47, He and His apostles said often. But I'm not sure you yet understand what I'm saying."

"Oh, I get what you are saying. You're saying that there's nothing more required than simple intellectual belief in Jesus' promise of eternal life to the one who believes in Him. You don't think that commitment to serve Him is required. Nor do you think that good works are needed. But if that were true, then why wouldn't people who believed in Jesus simply go out and live like the devil? You could have heaven and indulge the flesh all you want."

"That's right, Steve. Jesus promises eternal life to all who simply believe in Him. There are no strings attached. You can have heaven and indulge the flesh too. Of course, why anyone would want to live a miserable, painful life here and now makes no sense..."

How could I lead Steve to faith in Christ without telling him about the fact that Jesus guarantees *eternal life* to all who merely believe in Him? Assurance is standard equipment in the good news. Certainty is not optional equipment. You can't believe the gospel without knowing that as a result of believing it you have everlasting life.

I imagine at the Judgment Seat of Christ we will discover that millions of Christians came to faith in Christ *after* they were "led to Christ." They came to faith during "follow-up" when their friend explained assurance to them.

THE CONSEQUENCES OF SEPARATION

It's tragic to separate assurance and evangelism because then the gospel is not made clear until (and if) follow up occurs.

Let's say a person comes to faith in Jesus during follow up when he is told about assurance. But he believes that he was saved when he was evangelized and "received Jesus." When he evangelizes others he will most likely perpetuate that error.

A person with this view will feel that they have been clear in evangelism even if they don't mention assurance. Since they consider assurance part of follow up, it's optional in their minds.

People who separate assurance from evangelism tend to end their evangelistic presentation something like this: "If you receive Jesus, He will save you. You can receive Him right now by praying and inviting Him into your life. It isn't the prayer that saves. But prayer is a way of expressing your heart to God. Would you like to receive Him right now?" Then the person is led in a prayer.

Of course, I have a problem with calling someone to do anything other than believe in Jesus. Asking a person to receive Him is far from clear. Fuzzier still is asking someone to invite Christ into his life. However, as flawed as those appeals are, there's another major problem with this approach. It fails to make clear the promise of the gospel!

Notice that eternal security is not made clear. Everlasting life is not mentioned. To speak of *salvation* is confusing for most people today. Unless you make it crystal clear that what you mean is everlasting life, eternal security, most people will think you are speaking of what a friend of mine likes to call *provisional salvation*.

They will most likely think, "Okay, since I've invited Jesus into my life, I am saved *for now*. I'll *stay saved* if I follow Christ like I should." Such a person doesn't yet grasp the promise of the gospel.

Jesus doesn't promise *provisional salvation* or *provisional life*. He promises *everlasting life* to all who simply believe in Him. That's good news!

THREE ESSENTIALS

When Jesus evangelized, as seen in passages like John 3:16; 5:24; 6:47; and 11:25-27, He routinely communicated three things. We, too, must share those three elements. They are:

1. believing
2. in Jesus
3. for eternal life.

I like to put it together in one sentence as follows: *Jesus guarantees everlasting life* to all who simply *believe* in Him. All who simply believe in Jesus are eternally secure. There are no hidden terms. That's it.

If you don't mention Jesus, you haven't given enough information. How much detail you give on His substitutionary death (and His finished work) and resurrection depends on the time you have, the prior knowledge of the person you are talking with, and the flow of the conversation. However, to fail to mention Jesus is to drop the ball in evangelism.

Additionally, you must mention what it is that He promises: *eternal life* to all who simply *believe* in Him.

If you don't mention eternal life or the equivalent (salvation that can never be lost no matter what we do or don't do), you haven't given enough information. Jesus doesn't promise provisional salvation. No one is put on probation. God can't and won't take back eternal life once He gives it to us. Fail to make this clear and you haven't communicated the good news.

And if you don't mention that this eternal life is given to all who merely believe in Jesus, you haven't given sufficient information. We must be careful not to substitute words we think have the same basic meaning as believing, but which really don't.[1] Asking Him into one's life is not the same as believing in Him. Neither is committing one's life to Him. Believing in Him for eternal life is being convinced that He guarantees eternal life to all who simply believe in Him.

Won't It Offend Some?

A friend named Charles wrote and asked me if sharing eternal security as part of the gospel won't turn some people off. He said that when he witnessed, people didn't have much trouble accepting the fact that Jesus died for us and rose again. But once he started talking about eternal security, most people would disagree and take offense and he'd "lose them" as far as evangelism is concerned. He wondered if it wouldn't be better to lead them to faith first and then tell them about eternal security later.

I told Charles what I've told you here. We can't lead someone to faith without communicating eternal security since that is part of what we must believe. Eternal life is what Jesus promises. When people take offense and disagree, that's fine. It shows we are communicating clearly. Our goal isn't to convince people per se. That's really between them and God. We just share the message and leave the results up to God.

A person is not born again merely by believing that Jesus died on the cross for their sins and rose again.[2] Everyone in Christianity believes that. Even people in the cults believe that.

What makes a person a Christian is when they realize that Jesus, the One who died and rose again, guarantees everlasting life to all who simply believe in Him. Until they believe in eternal security, they've not yet understood the point of Calvary and the empty tomb.

Standard Equipment

The bottom line is that assurance is not optional in our evangelistic presentations. It's mandatory. If you don't convey the promise, which is the certainty (the assurance) that all who simply believe in Jesus have everlasting life, then you haven't conveyed the saving promise clearly.

I hope this book will motivate people who know they're eternally secure by faith alone in Christ alone to share that message with others every single time they evangelize. It would be great if people stopped treating assurance as some advanced Christian doctrine. This is part of the milk of the Word. Assurance is part of the saving message itself.

---

[1] Even the word *trust* is not necessarily the same as *belief*. We've all heard illustrations of people who *believe* a chair will hold them up, but they don't *trust* in the chair until they sit in it. Whatever trust is in that illustration, it is clearly more than belief! If trust and belief are actually synonymous, then a person can trust a chair to hold him up without actually sitting in it.

[2] Admittedly a proper understanding of *the finished work of Christ* on the cross includes the conviction that all who believe in Jesus are eternally secure. However, that underscores my point. You can't proclaim the finished work without proclaiming eternal security for all who believe in Christ.

~ Section 3 ~

OVERCOMING OBSTACLES

*Take heed to yourselves and
to all the flock, among which
the Holy Spirit has made you
overseers, to shepherd the church
of God which He purchased with
His own blood. For I know this,
that after my departure savage
wolves will come in among you,
not sparing the flock.*
Acts 20:28-29

— Chapter 10 —

WILL THE REAL CHRISTIAN
PLEASE STAND UP?

Do you believe that there is such a thing as a false profession of faith in Christ? I do. The reason is simple. Even a casual reading of the New Testament shows that there are people in Christianity who think and profess that they are on their way to the kingdom, but who are not. Such people are false professors.

But here's a tougher question. How do you recognize a false professor when you meet one?

Here's a clue. In a recent survey conducted by the Barna Research Group, over 6,000 American churchgoers were asked if a person could earn his way to heaven by doing good works. Amazingly 70 percent answered "Yes"![1]

The vast majority of people today do not believe that Jesus guarantees eternal life to all who simply believe in Him. It stands to reason, therefore, that a large number of "Christians" today are *false professors*, if by that expression we mean those who profess to believe in Jesus and yet in reality do not.

How, then, do we identify false professors?

FALSE PROFESSORS AND FALSE BRETHREN

Toward the end of the Sermon on the Mount, the Lord deals with the issue of false professors. He said,

> "Many will say to Me in that day, 'Lord, Lord, have we not prophesied in Your name, cast out demons in Your name, and done many wonders in Your name?' And then I will declare to them, 'I never knew you; depart from Me, you who practice lawlessness!'"
>
> —Matthew 7:21-23

We'll discuss *why* these people are false professors in a moment. But it's clear from this passage that there will be false professors at the judgment of unbelievers. These people will be making their case as to why they believe they should get into Jesus' kingdom. Yet Jesus tells us in advance that these people will not have their expectations met.

Paul taught something similar. He spoke of "false brethren" who secretly worked their way into the churches of Galatia in an effort to bring the believers there under the bondage of legalism (Galatians 2:4). These men did not believe or proclaim the apostolic gospel of justification by faith alone (see Galatians 1:6-9), but rather they taught justification by faith plus works (Galatians 3:1-5; 5:1-15).

It's likely that these false brethren initially pretended to agree with apostolic doctrine. Paul said they were "secretly brought in" and that they "came in by stealth" (Galatians 2:4). My guess is they didn't say something like, "Hi, we're here to show you that Paul is a heretic and that his view of the gospel won't save anyone." Quickly, however, their true colors emerged and they began trying to proselytize the believers of Galatia toward their works-salvation "gospel."

Today the situation is more complicated, for now we no longer have just one church in each city. Nor do all churches believe and teach the one true gospel. Thus when a person today says "I'm a Christian," or "I'm a follower of Christ," you can't be sure what they believe concerning the good news.

If people point to their works as the reason why they should get into the kingdom, their professions of faith are to be questioned (Matthew 7:21-23).

Those who compare themselves with others and suggest that their relative goodness proves their right standing with God show they don't believe the good news (Luke 18:9-14).

People who claim they deserve kingdom entrance because of their ancestry are also false professors (Luke 3:8).

Finally, if people point to their zeal for righteousness as proof they are born again, they are inadvertently testifying against themselves as well (Romans 10:2).

THE DANGER OF FAULTY TESTING

There are three commonly suggested tests for determining whether someone is a false professor[2]:

1. Consider the quality of his works.
2. Observe how grieved he is when he sins.

3.   Discern his desire to have an intimate relationship with God.[3]

The problem with such tests is threefold.

First, some *unbelievers* may appear to pass with flying colors. Some unbelievers are fervent in their efforts to do good works and live very moral lives. Many unbelievers are quite grieved over their sins. And lots of unbelievers have a very strong desire for holiness and an intimate relationship with God.

Second, some *believers* may do poorly on one or more of these tests. King David would have failed miserably during the first year after his fall with Bathsheba. Many of the believers in Corinth would also have come up short (cf. 1 Corinthians 3:1-3; 6:1-20; 11:30).

Third, and most importantly, the Scriptures do not validate the idea of using such tests (see, for example, Matthew 7:21-23; Luke 8:9-14; John 11:25-27; 1 Corinthians 6:12-20; Galatians 2:15-16).

Of course, there's a good reason why people try to measure the spiritual status of others through the use of tests such as these. Concern about holiness prompts people, reasonably enough, to focus on good works, sin, and one's desire to walk with God. The problem is not in the concern. Rather, it's in the application.

Paul expressed these very concerns in his first letter to the Corinthians. Yet not once did he question the born-again status of the readers. Even when he exhorted the Corinthians to turn from the immorality that existed among them, he *based* his appeal on their regenerate status:

> Do you not know that your bodies are members of Christ? Shall I then take members of Christ and make them members of a harlot? Certainly

not...Flee sexual immorality. Every sin that a man does is outside the body, but he who commits sexual immorality sins against his own body. Or do you not know that your body is the temple of the Holy Spirit who is in you, whom you have from God, and you are not your own?

— 1 Corinthians 6:15, 18-19.

DISCERNING FALSE PROFESSORS BIBLICALLY

Justification is by faith alone. And Paul tells us justification by faith apart from works *is* the good news (Galatians 2:15-16). Thus the *only* valid litmus test for determining who is a false professor is whether or not a person believes in justification by faith alone.

While the Lord Jesus rarely used the term *justification* (see Luke 18:9-14), He often spoke of eternal life as a free gift to all who simply believe in Him (see, for example, John 4:10-14; 6:35-40, 47; 11:25-27; 20:31; Revelation 22:17).

Thus everyone who claims to believe in Jesus and yet believes that faith in Him, apart from works, is not enough to be eternally secure, is a false professor. A false professor is one who claims to believe in Jesus yet who does not believe the saving message.

When asked why they think that they should get into heaven, many false professors will say something like this:

"Well, I've lived a decent life; I've tried hard to obey God; I pray and go to church and read my Bible; and I sincerely think that though I'm a sinner, I deserve to get in because I'm committed to God and it shows in what I've done with my life."

Have you ever heard someone say something like that? That's the way I thought until I understood and believed the grace of God as a senior in college.

Other false professors give a slightly different reason for their hope of heaven:

> "I know I'm a sinner and I don't deserve to get into the kingdom. However, as I look at my life, I see evidence of the work of the Spirit. The works that God is seemingly doing through me give me reason to believe I've been chosen by Him. Of course, I realize I may fall away in the future and prove I was never born again in the first place. However, if I continue on the path I'm on now, I have every reason to believe I'll make it."

I mentioned Matthew 7:21-23 above. Let's now look at it more carefully.

> "Not everyone who says to Me, 'Lord, Lord,' shall enter the kingdom of heaven, but he who does the will of My Father in heaven. Many will say to Me in that day, 'Lord, Lord, have we not prophesied in Your name, cast out demons in Your name, and done many wonders in Your name?' Then I will declare to them, 'I never knew you; depart from Me, you who practice lawlessness!'"

The phrase "in that day" ("Many will say to Me *in that day*," italics added) refers to the Great White Throne Judgment that will occur after the millennium (see Revelation 20:11-15), when all of the unsaved dead will have their day in God's court and receive their final judgment.

The people mentioned in Matthew 7:21-23 are not Buddhists or Hindus or Muslims. They are people from within

Christendom. Note they indicate three times that they have done good works "in Your name." With rare exceptions (like first-century Jewish exorcists casting out demons in Jesus' name), only "Christians" have attempted to do good works specifically *in Jesus' name*.

Jesus doesn't say, "I knew you, but then you fell away and lost eternal life." Instead He says, "I *never* knew you" (italics added). The reason why He never knew them is clear. These people did not do "the will of [Jesus'] Father." When we look at other passages in which that expression occurs, we find that the will of the Father is that we believe in His Son (see John 6:28-29, 38-40).

Some people think this way:

> "Well, I believe a person will make it to the kingdom if he believes in Jesus and perseveres in good works. Now if I'm wrong, and all that is required is faith in Jesus, then I'll get in anyway because I have both faith and works. I just have more than is required, that's all."

The problem with this view is that faith in Jesus is not faith that He *helps* us make it into the kingdom. *The person who believes that justification is by faith plus works does not believe in Jesus in the biblical sense!* He believes things about Jesus, some of which are true (e.g., He is God). But he doesn't believe that all who simply believe in Him have everlasting life that can never be lost. Biblically to believe in Jesus is not the conviction that faith plus works will get a person into God's kingdom. Faith in Jesus is the conviction that simply by believing in Him, apart from any works one might have done or might do in the future, a person is born again.

False professors will be confronted with their sinfulness ("you who practice lawlessness"). Of course, it's true that Jesus by His death on the cross has "take[n] away the sin of the world" (John 1:29; 1 John 2:2). In other words, Jesus at Calvary made everyone *savable*. He didn't give everyone eternal life. But by His death on the cross He made that possible for all who simply believe in Him.

Matthew 7:21-23 shows it's incorrect to understand unlimited atonement to mean that unbelievers die free of their sins. Being *savable* is not the same as being saved or free from your sins.

Only those sinners who have believed in Jesus gain eternal life and die free of their sins. All who fail to believe in Jesus will die *in their sins*. Jesus said, "If you do not believe that I am He, you will die in your sins" (John 8:24).[4]

The problem is linking one's expectation of kingdom entrance with works. Here's the type of answer that pleases the Lord:

> "I know You will let me into Your kingdom because You said, 'He who lives and believes in Me shall never die' (John 11:26). I believed in You for eternal life while I was still alive, and so I know I have everlasting life and I'll never die spiritually, for You keep all Your promises. My life was far from perfect. But that's not the point. The point is, You paid the complete payment for my sins, and You will fulfill Your promise to open Your kingdom to me and to all who have believed in You for eternal life."

Of course, no one at the Great White Throne Judgment will say that, because only unbelievers will be judged there.[5] Jesus promises that those who believe in Him "will not come into condemnation [literally, judgment]" (John 5:24). Believers will be judged, not to determine their eternal destiny, for that is a done deal (John 3:18; 5:24), but to determine their degrees of reward in the kingdom (2 Corinthians 5:9-10).

The two types of people we've just discussed both genuinely believe that they are Christians, or that it is likely that they are Christians. If you told these types of people that all who simply believe in Jesus have eternal life, they'd say that *you* weren't a Christian![6]

Yet there is another type of false professor. They believe a false gospel or even no gospel at all, but profess to believe the true gospel. If you told them that all who simply believe in Jesus have eternal life, they'd disingenuously voice agreement with you.

PEOPLE WHO OUTRIGHT LIE

If you make it a habit to ask people you have witnessed to if they believe what you've said, you will find that some of them will answer "Yes" who are not really convinced.

Some cultures are particularly sensitive about this issue to the point that a person will lie to you rather than risk offending you.

Others might answer "Yes" simply because it is a quick way to end an uncomfortable conversation.

Still others might falsely profess to believe what you say because they hope by doing so you will give them money (e.g., homeless people).

My suggestion is that if someone claims to believe the good news, then you should accept their profession as true, unless good reasons lead you to believe otherwise. Those reasons would not be fruit related, but root related.

The root is the foundation of a tree. In this case the root illustrates what someone believes. The fruit refers to the production of a tree. In the case of a false professor, the fruit illustrates the good works he does or doesn't do.

Well, you can't identify a false professor by his fruit. What he does may not give an accurate picture of what he believes. Some believers struggle in terms of their words and deeds. Some unbelievers are wonderfully charismatic people and appear to have it all together.

The only accurate way to determine if someone believes the true gospel is to find out what they believe.

If you hear, for example, that a person you spoke with and who professed to believe in Jesus alone for eternal life is now telling others that you are a religious fanatic and that they agreed with you to get rid of you, that's strong evidence they falsely professed faith. They are testifying about what they believe. It's a root question, not a fruit question.

LET YOUR LIGHT SHINE

I was on a plane seated next to a lady who was reading her Bible. I asked her if she was a Christian. She said she was. I shared with her my burden for the purity of the gospel. I told her about faith alone in Christ alone as compared with *faith-plus* gospels. It was obvious, based on her lack of positive response, she didn't agree with me. She quickly changed the subject to Christian issues with which she was more comfortable. She clearly wasn't comfortable with the idea of justification by faith alone, apart from works. I was glad I shared the saving message with her. My prayer is that she would come to faith.

It's possible, of course, for a person who once believed in Christ for eternal life to become confused. Even though he has eternal life, he no longer realizes it.

Confused believers need to hear the clear gospel again, for they have forgotten the simple message of eternal life. They need a reminder to regain the assurance they once had.

False professors are out there. If, as the Barna study shows, seventy percent of churchgoers in America today believe that people can earn their way to heaven, then nearly three-fourths of all professing Christians are false professors. Keep in mind, however, that there are many who would answer "No" to that question who nonetheless believe that faith in Jesus is not enough. They are simply not comfortable speaking of people who earn their way to heaven by good works. This would drive the percentage of false professors much higher.

The reason why so few "Christians" today have assurance is because of the widespread confusion about what one must do to have eternal life. Most church people today will either specifically say it takes faith plus works, or that all it takes is faith, but the faith must be some special *kind* of faith that results in persevering good works. Even in this latter case, faith in Jesus is not enough. Good works must be added "to prove one *truly* believed in Jesus in the first place."

I trust you know that you are a true professor. If so, this book is for you. It will help you stay sure and it will help you help others who aren't sure.

If you aren't sure whether your profession is true, this book is for you as well. It will help you become sure. Only when you yourself are sure can you have the foundation needed to live a godly life and to evangelize others.

It's really simple. Jesus promises eternal life to all who merely believe in Him. Once you believe that, you're sure. You don't need to massage what Jesus said and add the kitchen sink into what it means to believe in Him. He didn't. In terms of having eternal life, He didn't speak of believing and committing and turning from sins and doing good works. He said that all who simply believe in Him have everlasting life. That is bedrock that will hold you forever.

---

[1] "Religious Beliefs Vary Widely By Denomination," *The Barna Update* (June 25, 2001): http://www.barna.org. The article states, "Just three out of every ten Americans [who attend church] embrace the traditional Protestant perspective that good works cannot earn a person salvation."

[2] Darrell Bock, "A Review of *The Gospel According to Jesus*," *Bibliotheca Sacra* (Jan-Mar 1989): pp. 31-32.

[3] The number of tests people suggest varies greatly. I've seen some suggest as many as eleven tests. However, these three tests are fairly representative. In the case of everyone who advocates such tests, they view perseverance in faith and good works as necessary in order for a person to make it to heaven.

[4] What does it mean to die in your sins (John 8:24) or in your sin, singular (John 8:21)? The Bible is not clear on this question. I think it means that unbelievers die with sinful desires. It might also mean that unbelievers will be judged for their sins at the Great White Throne Judgment. Even though their unbelief is the basis of their condemnation (John 3:18; Revelation 20:15), their sins will be judged and they will receive degrees of suffering forever in keeping with their sins (Revelation 20:11-13). While believers will be judged for all their deeds, good and bad (2 Corinthians 5:10), they will not be judged for their sins. For believers, bad deeds will be judged as deeds, not as sins.

[5] Of course it is hypothetically possible that people who came to faith in Jesus during the Millennium will also be judged at the Great White Throne Judgment. If so, the purpose of their judgment would be to determine their degree of reward on the new earth in the eternal kingdom. After all, John 3:18 and 5:24 would still apply to them. There is no indication in Scripture of when millennial believers will be judged. Revelation 20:15 ("anyone not found written in the Book of Life") may imply that others are being judged there. Or it may simply mean that others will be present, such as church-age believers who will serve as witnesses.

[6] Both types believe that perseverance in good works is necessary for kingdom entrance. Since you deny that, they say *you* don't believe the gospel!

— Chapter 11 —

WHY NOT LIVE LIKE THE DEVIL?

First Timothy 4:8

An atheist who loved nature went camping. Rising before dawn, he walked to a breathtaking vista to watch the sun rise. A thousand feet below him lay a beautiful canyon. As he stood near the edge of the canyon wall, the soil beneath him gave way, plunging him over the edge. Wildly he grasped for something to deliver him from sure death. Miraculously he caught a branch growing out of the canyon wall. Here he hung, awaiting his demise. He knew he couldn't hold on for long. And there was no one within miles to hear his cries for help.

Suddenly this atheist began to reconsider. *Maybe I'm really an agnostic.* He looked toward the heavens and cried out, "Is anybody up there?"

To his amazement a voice replied, "Yes, I'm here. Why do you call on Me?"

"What should I do?"

"Let go of the branch."

Aghast, he thought for a moment and asked, "Is *anyone else* up there?"

That story hits closer to home than most of us would care to admit. God tells us what to do and if it doesn't make sense to us, then we want a second opinion.

Have you ever shared the gospel with someone and received resistance over the idea that simply by believing in Jesus we can be absolutely sure that we are eternally secure? "If I'm sure I'm saved forever, then why wouldn't I just go out and live as I please?" is a question many of us have often heard.

How do you answer that? Often we aren't as well prepared as we should be to deal with this candid query. Fortunately, in 1 Timothy 4:8 the apostle Paul provides two powerful reasons why eternally secure believers should obey God and not seek a second opinion.

GODLINESS IS PROFITABLE IN THIS LIFE

Paul begins verse 8 by contrasting godliness with bodily exercise: "For bodily exercise profits a little..." For the last seven years I've been somewhat of an exercise fanatic, racewalking an average of a thousand miles per year. In addition, I swim and ride an exercise bike. A daily regimen of exercise helps me think better, sleep better, feel better, and hopefully live longer. Yet in comparison to the development of godliness (spiritual exercise, if you will), physical exercise has limited benefit.[1]

Paul continues: "…godliness is profitable for all things, having promise of the life that now is…" Do you believe that? Are you confident that the only way to be truly happy, content, and successful is to be a godly person?

Let's be honest. Sometimes it's a difficult concept to buy, isn't it?

Many Christians would argue that the verse should read: "*wickedness…*[has] promise of the life that now is." Nice guys finish last. The meek may inherit the earth, but not any time soon.

But God's Word is true, and obeying Him is always in our best interest—whether we believe it or not!

The corollary is also true: sin never pays.

Remember Kurt Cobain? Marilyn Monroe? Tupac Shakur? John Belushi? All of them died at a young age due in great part to their sinful lifestyles.

In 1972 President Richard Nixon authorized a break-in at the Democratic National Headquarters in Watergate. Then when the thieves were arrested, he authorized a cover-up using illegal funds. Finally he resigned in disgrace, his life shattered because of ungodly behavior.

In 1988 Senator Gary Hart was the frontrunner for the Presidency, but when his extramarital affair became public knowledge, he was forced to drop out of the race in humiliation.

Magic Johnson is one of the greatest basketball players to ever live. Yet on November 7, 1991 he was forced to quit in his prime, after he contracted AIDS as a result of a promiscuous lifestyle. That lifestyle caused him to cut short not only his NBA career, but probably his life as well.

Stories of people whose lives were hurt and even ruined by sin are endless. The point is: sin never pays. Obedience always does.

Need more corroboration? First Timothy 4:8 gives a second reason why those who are assured of their eternal destiny should be highly motivated to live for God.

GODLINESS IS PROFITABLE FOR THE LIFE TO COME

Paul continues, "Godliness is profitable for...the life...which is to come." Remember that Paul was writing to Timothy who was already a believer—a "true son in the faith" (1 Timothy 1:2). The subject here is not kingdom entrance, but rewards in the next life. Actually Paul wrote much to Timothy about laying hold of eternal rewards (compare 1 Timothy 6:6, 14, 19; 2 Timothy 1:12; 2:3-6, 12, 15; 4:6-10).

In 1 Timothy 4:8, Paul is saying that the lives of believers consist of two parts. The first part is composed of our present lives of maybe 80 to 100 years at best, when we must contend with the sinful inclinations of our flesh and bodies that decay, suffer pain, injuries, etc.

Once we die or are raptured, our eternal life takes on a new form. Like a butterfly emerging from a cocoon, our born-of-God selves appear in their glorified beauty. No more pain, suffering, or sin.

Paul is concerned here with our lives after we are resurrected and are in the kingdom. Eternally-secure people would do well to heed Paul's reminder to Timothy that godliness will make life better in the life to come. Though the life to come will be a beautiful experience for all believers, this verse makes it clear that everyone will not enjoy the same level of joy, fulfillment, and privileges. The degree to which one will experience the joys of the kingdom is directly related to how much godliness he developed in this life. Godliness now means a larger capacity to serve and glorify Him then.

Jesus said in John 10:10, "I came that you might have life, and that you might have it *more abundantly*" (emphasis added). That is true now and forever.

Hebrews 11 records the abundant lives of Noah, Abraham, Sarah, Moses, Joseph, Rahab, Gideon, Samson, David, and Samuel. The author tells us that they will obtain "a better resurrection" (Hebrews 11:35).[2] That *better resurrection* is a more abundant experience in the life to come.[3]

New Testament Hall of Famers who persevered in faith and good works include the twelve apostles, Paul, Barnabas, James, Jude, Mary, Joseph, Elizabeth, Zacharias, Simeon, and Anna. All of these believers will have more abundant experiences in the life to come. So too, any believer who perseveres will have a more abundant eternal experience.

GODLINESS IS THE ONLY SENSIBLE WAY TO LIVE

For the person who is sure he has eternal life, Paul gives two powerful motivations for obedience: profit in this life and profit in the life to come. What more is there than that? Only fools would pursue anything other than godliness if they count Paul's counsel as trustworthy.

The simple reason why many people believe that certainty would produce sinful lifestyles is because they don't believe what

God says about godliness and sinfulness. They don't believe that godliness produces joy and wellness. Nor do they believe that sinfulness produces pain and illness.

God has spoken clearly. We need to let go of our efforts to merit eternal life. Letting go of that branch may not make sense to us in terms of the way *we* would construct the gospel. But it sure should make total sense to us since it is *God* who determines what we must do to have eternal life.

If God tells us to let go of our self-righteous attitudes and actions, then that is what we should do. It makes sense, for God indeed knows what we must do to have eternal life.

And when we believe in Jesus for eternal life, we will find that instead of falling into the canyon of sin and degradation, we will be highly motivated to rise to holiness and fullness of life.

---

[1] If bodily exercise enables us to serve God better, then we will be more highly rewarded in the life to come as a result. Thus bodily exercise can have limited value both for this life and the life to come.

[2] While Hebrews 11:35 directly concerns those unnamed believers who are tortured and even martyred for their faith, it surely applies to *all* those mentioned specifically by name as well.

[3] Some think the better resurrection is the first resurrection, that is, kingdom entrance. That is impossible for then Hebrews 11:35 would teach justification by martyrdom!

— Chapter 12 —

CONTEMPLATING APPROVAL
Second Corinthians 13:5

God commands Christians to examine ourselves. If we are wise, we assess all areas of our lives including our church involvement, job, family, giving, prayer life, spending, health, etc. Even if God didn't tell us to examine how we are doing in our service for Christ, it makes perfect sense that we do so regularly.

The apostle Paul admonished the believers at Corinth to do this very thing when he wrote:

> Examine yourselves as to whether you are in the faith. Test yourselves. Do you not know yourselves, that Jesus Christ is in you?—unless indeed you are disqualified.
>
> —2 Corinthians 13:5

While self-evaluation is obviously taught in Scripture, the *purpose* of that examination is not necessarily obvious. Two major views exist in the church today regarding the purpose of self-examination. Some say its purpose is to give us assurance that we are truly born again. Others say its purpose is to help those who are certain they have eternal life to be (or remain) on course to obtain Christ's approval at the Judgment Seat of Christ.

There are a number of compelling proofs in Second Corinthians itself that demonstrate that the purpose of this self-examination was not evangelistic. Paul was seeking to move regenerate people to be humble followers of Christ. He was not trying to lead false professors to faith in Christ.

PAUL AFFIRMED ASSURANCE
APART FROM WORKS

Paul was writing to believers, a fact he repeatedly asserted throughout both First and Second Corinthians. Nine times in these two epistles he referred to the fact that his readers had faith in Christ (1 Corinthians 2:5; 3:5; 15:2, 11, 14, 17; 16:13; 2 Corinthians 1:24; 10:15). He affirmed this in spite of the fact that the believers in Corinth were guilty of a number of significant moral failings. They had been plagued with divisions, strife, envy, drunkenness, and immorality (1 Corinthians 1:11; 3:1-3; 5:9–6:20; 11:21, 30). Their works certainly didn't prove they were saved. In fact, according to Paul, they were "behaving like mere men," that is, like the unsaved (1 Corinthians 3:3).

Paul referred to the carnal behavior of the believers at Corinth, and yet he called them "babes in Christ" (1 Corinthians 3:1-3). When chastising them about immorality, he reminded them that their bodies were "temple[s] of the Holy Spirit" (1 Corinthians 6:19). In spite of their immature behavior, he affirmed their eternal security.

Paul didn't want his readers to doubt their salvation, but to live in light of the fact that they were secure children of God. His appeals to live righteously were built upon their assurance that they were born again. To understand 2 Corinthians 13:5, we must take into account that Paul did not link their assurance to works but to faith in Christ.

ABIDING IN THE CHRISTIAN FAITH

The fact that Paul commands the readers to test themselves for the purpose of seeing if they are "in the faith" is seen by many as compelling proof that the issue here is justification.

While it is true that in a positional sense all believers are "in the faith," that does not mean that Paul is here thinking of the *position* of his readers. Indeed, the entire context concerns their *experience*, not their position.

Paul used the expression *in the faith* four times in his letters. All four times the expression refers to the believer's *experience*, not his position.

Paul always used this expression in conjunction with imperatives. In the three uses outside of 2 Corinthians 13:5, he commanded believers to "stand fast in the faith" (1 Corinthians 16:13), to "be sound in the faith" (Titus 1:13), and to be "established in the faith" (Colossians 2:7).[1] "The faith" is the body of truth that has been delivered to us from God.

There is compelling reason to conclude that Paul was exhorting his spiritual charges to obey in their experience that teaching which they had received. In *The Bible Knowledge Commentary*, Dave Lowery comments:

> Paul's question is usually construed with regard to positional justification: were they Christians or not? But it more likely concerned practical sanctification: did they *demonstrate* that they were in the faith (cf. 1 Cor 16:13) and that Christ was in them by their obeying His will? To stand the test was to do what was right. To fail was to be disobedient and therefore subject to God's discipline.[2]

CHRIST ABIDES IN BELIEVERS WHO ABIDE IN HIM

The purpose of this self-examination is also stated to be a determination of whether "Christ [is] in you." This phrase could refer to something true of all regenerate people since Christ lives in all believers.

However, in Scripture "Christ in you" is associated with progressive sanctification. For example, after saying, "You are already clean because of the word which I have spoken to you" (John 15:3), Jesus commanded the apostles to abide in Him so that He might abide in them (John 15:4). In order for Christ to abide in the believer, the believer must abide in Christ. Christ is at home in the lives of believers only if they openly and honestly obey Him.

In this context the abiding ministry of Jesus in the believer is most naturally understood as an issue related to progressive sanctification, not justification. It is reasonable to challenge believers to examine their works to see if Christ is abiding in them.

DISQUALIFICATION APPLIES TO BELIEVERS ONLY

The term *disqualified* (Greek: *adokimos*) occurs three times in 2 Corinthians 13:5-7. Most, if not all, of its other New Testament uses refer to *believers* who fail to gain Christ's approval. *Adokimos* means "disapproved." Its antonym, *dokimos*, occurs in the AWANA[3] verse, 2 Timothy 2:15, "Be diligent to present yourself *approved* to God, a worker who does not need to be ashamed, rightly dividing the word of truth" (italics added). *Approval* and *disapproval* are terms related to the Judgment Seat of Christ. Believers whose lives have been pleasing to Christ will be approved, while believers whose lives have displeased Christ will be disapproved. Rewards will be given to those who receive the Lord's approval, His "Well done."[4]

Acceptance and approval are two different things. God accepts all believers solely on the basis of their faith in Christ. Once they come to faith in Christ, they are forever accepted. Approval requires more than faith. It is conditioned upon spiritual maturity and is not a once-for-all event. A believer who is approved today is not guaranteed approval this time next year. Remaining in a state of Christ's approval is contingent upon being a spiritual believer (1 Corinthians 2:14).

Paul used *adokimos* in only one other place in First and Second Corinthians. There he indicated his fear that *he himself* might be disapproved by Christ at His Judgment Seat: "But I discipline my body and bring it into subjection, lest, when I have preached to others, I myself should become *disqualified*" (1 Corinthians 9:27, italics added). Paul knew that he was eternally secure. What he feared was Christ's disapproval.[5]

In 2 Corinthians 13:5, Paul challenged the believers at Corinth to examine themselves to see if they were approved or disapproved. In verse 6 he reminded them that he and his fellow missionaries were not disapproved, although he acknowledged in verse 7 that they might *seem* disapproved to some in the Corinthian church. In other words, Paul knew that he was currently living in such a way as to merit Christ's approval. This he could not affirm of the believers at Corinth, for there was plenty of evidence to suggest otherwise.

Examination of our works to see if we can rightfully expect Christ's approval at His Judgment Seat is completely consistent with Paul's teachings elsewhere in First and Second Corinthians (see 1 Corinthians 3:10-15; 9:24-27; 2 Corinthians 5:9-10) and in his other letters as well (see Romans 14:10-13; Galatians 5:19-21; 6:7-9; Ephesians 5:5-7; Philippians 3:11-14; Colossians 1:21-23; 2 Timothy 2:12, 15). We should always be living in light of the fact that Jesus might come back today. According to Paul, approval or disapproval by Christ will be based on how we live. Self-examination is an important discipline that helps us be prepared to receive Christ's approval.

DOES GOD APPROVE OF YOU?

The Scriptures challenge us as Christians to examine ourselves to determine how we are doing in our individual walks with Christ. Are we delighting Him by our lives? Does He approve of us? Or, are we living for the praise and approval of others? Is our mind conformed to God's Word or to the world?

Self-examination can help us prepare for the Judgment Seat of Christ. If we are ready, we will hear those words of approval, "Well done, good servant" (Luke 19:17).

Examining our works is not an *assurance* issue. We know we have eternal life because we believe the promise of eternal life to all who simply believe in Jesus. Self-examination plays no role in that.

Self-examination is an *approval* issue. We know that we will have Jesus' approval if we persevere in a life of faith and good works. The abundance of our eternal experience depends on what we do with the life God has given us. If we live each day in light of the Judgment Seat of Christ, then we will have the mindset needed to persevere and to rule with Christ in the life to come.

But what if we fail to persevere? The next chapter directly addresses that question.

---

[1] Note that these three commands are to believers, not to a mix of true and false professors. We should thus be inclined to see the remaining command concerning "in the faith" (2 Corinthians 13:5) as directed to born-again people as well.

[2] David K. Lowery, "Second Corinthians" in *The Bible Knowledge Commentary*, New Testament Edition, eds. John Walvoord and Roy Zuck (Wheaton, IL: Victor Books, 1983), pp. 584-85, italics original.

[3] AWANA stands for Approved Workmen Are Not Ashamed. AWANA is an international children's ministry. Local churches which adopt the program receive excellent materials and training in how to evangelize and disciple children.

[4] Note that Christ's approval is not guaranteed to those who believe in Him. His approval is only for those believers who "rightly divide the word of truth" and who are effective "workers" for Christ. Clearly the issue in 2 Timothy 2:15 is not justification, but sanctification and eternal rewards.

[5] I have actually met pastors who are five-point Calvinists who interpret Paul to be saying in 1 Corinthians 9:27 that he feared he might end up in hell! However, it is impossible that a person who knew he was an apostle of Jesus Christ (1 Corinthians 1:1) could at the same time doubt whether he had eternal

life. God didn't make unbelievers apostles. Paul knew if he died he would be with the Lord (2 Corinthians 5:8; Philippians 1:21). He also knew that his own name was in the Book of Life along with that of his coworkers (see Philippians 4:3).

— Chapter 13 —

WHAT IF WE FAIL TO PERSEVERE?

The Bible clearly calls believers to persevere in faith and good works. Indeed, this should be our aim in life. Paul said, *"I discipline my body and bring it into subjection,* lest, when I have preached to others, I myself should become disqualified" (1 Corinthians 9:27, italics added). Elsewhere he said, *"If we endure,* we shall also reign with Him" (2 Timothy 2:12, italics added). The Lord Jesus said, *"He who overcomes and keeps My works until the end,* to him I will give power over the nations" (Revelation 2:26, italics added). It's impossible to ignore the fact that perseverance is commanded, expected, and pleasing to God in order to be qualified for service now, and to reign with Christ in the future.

That's all well and good, but you may wonder why a book on assurance needs a chapter on perseverance. The reason is simple.

Many people consider perseverance to be the indispensable proof that one is born again.

Some believe that failure to persevere in a life of faith and good works proves a person was never born again in the first place. Others believe that failure to persevere causes a person to lose the eternal life they once had!

As long as a person thinks that perseverance is required to get into the kingdom, there is no assurance. He will be continually uncertain of his spiritual condition, for it's impossible to know for sure that he will persevere until he dies.

PERSEVERANCE IS A COMMAND, NOT A GUARANTEE

If God guarantees that all believers will persevere in faith and good works, why would the apostle Paul fear that he might not persevere (1 Corinthians 9:27)? Was the apostle to the Gentiles and author of half of the New Testament uncertain of his spiritual condition? Was Paul worried that he might end up spending eternity in hell? Obviously such suggestions are ridiculous.

If perseverance is guaranteed, the warnings in Scripture against failing to persevere don't make sense. The warnings prove that believers can fail to persevere. This life is a testing ground for the life to come. The Lord wishes for believers to prove themselves worthy of ruling in His kingdom (Revelation 3:4-5). If we persevere, we will win what Paul calls a "prize," which he further identifies as "an imperishable crown" (1 Corinthians 9:24-25).

Perseverance is about winning the Lord's *approval*, not His *acceptance*. He accepted us as His children when we believed in

Him for eternal life. We can never lose that. But we will only enjoy His approval if we live our lives (by faith) in obedience to His commands. And if we are faithfully serving Him when our earthly lives end, then we will experience His ultimate approval—rulership in His eternal kingdom.

PRESENT WELLNESS AND FUTURE RULERSHIP

While eternal life can never be lost, there are many negative consequences both now and in the life to come for the believer who fails to persevere in faith and good works.

One obvious but overlooked consequence is loss of abundant life here and now. Only believers walking in fellowship with God are joyful and content. Non-persevering saints are under God's discipline and until they repent, their misery will continue to escalate (Luke 15:11-24).

Our failure to persevere impacts everyone around us. Our spouses, children, neighbors, coworkers, and friends are impeded by our failure. Even total strangers can fall victim to the rage of a believer who is in rebellion against God.

I grew up in an alcoholic family. My father loved me dearly, but most of the time he was very difficult to be around. I realize now that he drank to cover his pain, thinking that liquor made him mellow. That couldn't have been further from the truth. Liquor made him belligerent. He rarely realized the pain and suffering he inflicted, especially on those who were closest to him.

According to my aunt, when my dad was a teen he believed in Jesus for eternal salvation. If that is true, then my dad was a believer who had strayed for a very long time. By the time I came along, he no longer believed the clear gospel. If he is with the Lord now, he illustrates the pain a non-persevering saint endures and passes on to those around him.

In terms of the life to come, believers who don't persevere will miss out on ruling with Christ, for that's a privilege reserved only for those who are faithful to the end. That is a tragedy of immense proportion. Too many believers don't realize how wonderful it will be to rule with Christ in the life to come. If they grasped it, they would live differently now.

In addition, there are other privileges which only persevering believers will experience in eternity. Let's consider those now.

OTHER ETERNAL REWARDS FOR ENDURING

For the believer who perseveres there will be other privileges in the life to come besides ruling with Christ. These will include wearing special white garments (Revelation 3:4-5), eating life-enhancing foods (the 12 fruits of the tree of life and the hidden manna, Revelation 2:7, 17; 22:14), having a white stone with an engraved name only you and the Lord Jesus know (Revelation 2:17), and having the right to enter the New Jerusalem by its gates (the places of honor in the Old Testament, Revelation 22:14).

Everyone longs for approval, especially from parents. Yet the greatest approval of all will be that of the Lord Jesus. How wonderful it would be to hear Him say, "Well done, good servant" (Luke 19:17).

Those who believe that perseverance is required to enter the kingdom are in bondage to a way of thinking that makes assurance impossible prior to death. And not knowing where you are going until after you die is a bad thing, for at that point there won't be anything you can do about it.

Perseverance is commanded. And rewards are promised to those believers who persevere. The fact that eternal life is guaranteed, whether we persevere or not, in no way lessens the rewards or cheapens the grace of God. We don't buy our way into the kingdom by perseverance in good works. That is a gift of God's *unmerited favor*.

— Chapter 14 —

FRACTURED FAITH

a·pos·ta·sy: *Abandonment of one's religious faith, a political party, one's principles, or a cause.*

At the tender age of 20, I cast my first vote. I voted for an ultra liberal presidential candidate. Given my socialist leanings at the time, I probably would have voted for a member of the American Communist Party if he or she had run. Today I am so conservative that I can hardly find any politicians that are conservative enough for me. It would appear, based on the above definition, that I have been guilty of political apostasy.

Day in and day out our beliefs are challenged, refined, and sometimes completely upended. We are not shocked when people change their beliefs about secular matters. We expect that. However, we are rightly shocked when people we know as fellow Christians abandon a fundamental Christian doctrine, or worse yet, completely abandon the Christian faith.

Christian apostasy leads to questions that are directly related to assurance. Is it possible for born-again people to stop believing one or more fundamental doctrines? Do people who commit apostasy lose eternal life or prove they were never born again in the first place?

If we haven't studied the Bible for answers to these questions, our own assurance may well vanish. We can't be sure that we ourselves will persevere in the faith. If apostasy disproves the new birth, then certainty this side of the grave is a myth.

DOES APOSTASY DISPROVE REGENERATION?

Those who believe that apostates were never truly born again rest their case on three primary arguments. The first is that saving faith is a gift of God and as such, is irrevocable. Therefore, it is impossible for a true believer to lose his faith.

The second argument is that saving faith is a unique *kind* of faith. While all other kinds of faith can fail, they believe this God-given supernatural faith cannot fail because of its very nature.

The third argument is that certain Scriptures are thought to make a case against the possibility of apostasy for the regenerate.

Let's briefly consider these three proofs.

Concerning the first proof, Ephesians 2:8-9 teaches that *salvation*, not faith, is a gift of God. We find that same truth in John 4:10; Romans 3:24; and Revelation 22:17. While it is true that no one comes to faith until God opens his heart and removes the satanic blinders (Acts 16:14; 2 Corinthians 4:4), it is not true that unbelievers are by nature unable to believe the saving message. The Bible doesn't teach this.[1]

The second proof, that saving faith is a unique kind of faith, is foreign to Scripture. Nowhere do we find the Lord Jesus or His apostles teaching that principle. Biblically, what makes saving faith *saving* is its unique object (Jesus, the One who guarantees eternal life to all who simply believe in Him), not the faith.

The third proof, the scriptural one, doesn't withstand scrutiny. Let's consider one proof text often used: "But the ones on the rock are those who, when they hear, receive the word with joy; and these have no root, who believe for a while and in time of temptation fall away" (Luke 8:13). I believe it actually proves that genuine believers may well apostatize. That verse is a warning against apostasy, not a statement that it is impossible.

The second soil in the Parable of the Four Soils represents those who believe the saving message, but in time of temptation fall away and cease believing. Make no mistake here. The message believed is clearly the saving message. In Luke 8:12 Jesus said that the reason why Satan snatches away the seed is because if anyone believes it, he will be saved. The very next verse, verse 13, speaks of those who believe that message. Thus according to Jesus' words in verse 12, the second soil represents born-again people.

Luke 8:13 doesn't prove that apostasy is impossible. It proves just the opposite.

Look at it this way—there is no time requirement as to how long you must believe in Jesus before you are eternally secure. The moment you believe, you are secure forever. That is why Satan is so energetically working to keep people from coming to faith. Once a person believes, Satan knows that he is God's forever.

The idea of apostasy is found in the writings of Paul and the epistle to the Hebrews as well. Paul spoke of those who "concerning the faith have suffered shipwreck" (1 Timothy 1:19).[2] He also spoke of those "who have strayed concerning the truth" (2 Timothy 2:18).[3] The author of Hebrews warned Jewish believers not to "fall away...and put [Jesus] to an open shame" (Hebrews 6:6).

Clearly a born-again person is not immune to apostasy. However, Jesus' promise holds true. Once we partake of the bread of life, that is, once we believe in Him, we "will never hunger" (John 6:35a). The one who "lives and believes in [Jesus] shall never die" (John 11:26).

Jesus linked this promise of eternal life to His Father's will. He said in John 6:39-40,

> This is the will of the Father who sent Me, that of all He has given Me *I should lose nothing, but should raise it up at the last day.* And this is the will of Him who sent Me, that everyone who sees the Son and believes in Him may have everlasting life; and I will raise him up at the last day (italics added).

If *anyone* who believed in Jesus ever failed to make it into the kingdom, then Jesus will have failed to do the will of the Father! It isn't that we need to stay faithful to keep eternal life. It is that *He needs to stay faithful* for us to keep it. And, of course, He will and He must (compare 2 Timothy 2:13).

Once a person believes in Jesus, he is secure forever. There is nothing, absolutely nothing, a born-again person can do to cause himself to lose everlasting life, or to prove he never had it.

We are not regenerated because we have eternal faith. We are born again because the Savior promised that the moment we believe in Him, we are eternally secure. Faith in an unfailing Savior guarantees eternal life even if the faith later fails.

Apostasy Is Possible for Believers

Here are a few reasons why apostasy is possible for born-again people:

First, *Christians aren't robots.* God didn't have androids in mind when He created man. We are in His image, but because of the fall, we are not perfect. Therefore, failure is possible.

Second, *Christians have minds and are capable of changing them.* How many times have you changed your mind about something? I've changed my mind about many doctrines during my 30-plus years as a believer. While I haven't apostatized, I could have. I still might. Continued belief in the fundamentals of the faith is reasonable, logical, normal, and desirable. But it isn't automatic.

Third, *God has chosen not to make apostasy impossible for believers.* This life is a test for us. Those who persevere in their confession of faith in Christ will be rulers in the life to come. Those who fail will not (see 2 Timothy 2:12 and Luke 19:11-27). If God were to remove the possibility of defection, then He would also be removing the test.

Fourth, *there are three major enemies we must battle until death: the world, the flesh, and the devil.* We live in a world that is currently dominated by Satan. The ideas of Hollywood, the media, and the academic elite are hostile to faith in Christ. Our bodies are fallen. As a result of Adam and Eve's sin, we have inherited sinful dispositions. Until we put off the flesh in which we live and gain glorified bodies free from sinful inclinations, we will have to battle the flesh. And the devil doesn't stop battling once a person comes to faith in Christ. At that point his aim shifts. He seeks to derail us and our testimony. Satan loves it when believers apostatize.

All three of our enemies will be powerless over us after we die or are raptured. Then we shall be just like Jesus in terms of our sinlessness (1 John 3:2). However, prior to our putting off these bodies, the possibility of defeat by our three enemies is very real.

TAKE HEED LEST YOU FALL

Pride comes before a fall. If you are convinced that you would never fall away from the faith, then you are more likely to fall.

Of course, if you're sure you have eternal life, then why would you fear apostasy? There are several reasons.

First, if you lose your faith, you lose your assurance. While eternal life cannot be lost, certainty can be.

Second, only those who endure in their faith in Christ will rule with Him in the life to come (Matthew 10:32; 2 Timothy 2:12; Hebrews 10:23-25).

Third, it is impossible to experience the abundant life now, and in the life to come, if we fall away from the faith (1 Timothy 4:8).

Fourth, if we are truly grateful for the shed blood of Christ that made our eternal security possible, then we will be highly motivated to please Him. We will want to hear Him say, "Well done, good and faithful servant." His approval will mean much to us.

So how do we avoid apostasy? There are some biblical admonitions that can keep us from straying. We are commanded to feed on God's Word, attend solid Bible-teaching churches, and pray without ceasing. However, if we do those things legalistically, we may well find they become drudgeries. If our Christian lives are to be joyful, we must have our constant focus on our soon returning Savior, Lord, and Judge. It is the love of Christ that must compel us (2 Corinthians 5:14). The Christian life is all about finding our joy in Jesus.

We should take comfort in the fact that nothing, not even apostasy, can cause us to miss the kingdom.

There is a day coming when apostasy will no longer occur. But that day is not here yet. Until it is, we must guard against apostasy. Continue to assemble with like-minded believers. Study God's Word and thereby have your mind renewed (Romans 12:2). And always look to Jesus who died for us and rose again and is coming again soon.

---

[1] For verses showing that unregenerate people have the ability to believe in Jesus, see, for example, Matthew 23:37; John 4:10 (asking for the saving message, not for faith); 7:17; Acts 10:44; 16:14.

[2] That Paul chose the figure of shipwreck is telling. Obviously, a person couldn't suffer shipwreck unless he was on a ship when the shipwreck occurred. Likewise, someone couldn't suffer shipwreck of his faith unless he actually had faith in the first place. Paul's comment in 1 Timothy 1:19 would be nonsense if he was referring to people who never believed in the first place.

[3] Again, it is significant that Paul spoke of those "who have strayed concerning the truth." Compare 1 Timothy 1:6 and 6:21, the only other places in the New Testament where the word *astocheō*, straying (or departing from), appears. In both of those verses as well, Paul refers to straying from the faith. Clearly, a person cannot stray from something unless he was originally in the fold. A person can't stray from the Christian faith without first believing the Christian faith. Unbelievers can't stray from the faith since they never had faith in the first place.

— Chapter 15 —

TESTING FIRST JOHN

Probably no portion of Scripture is more often cited as a proof text for assurance of salvation than First John. Commentator Robert Law first popularized the view that First John contains a series of tests that can be useful in helping a person determine if he or she has eternal life. This *tests of life* view makes sense only if you believe that assurance is something less than certainty and that it is based, not on what we believe, but on what we do. Unfortunately, many commentators understand First John in this way.

YOU CAN'T HAVE ASSURANCE BY WORKS

The list that follows is drawn from a recent book on assurance whose author holds the *tests of life* understanding of First John.[1] It contains some suggested criteria for determining if you are born again:

1. Have you enjoyed fellowship with Christ and with the Father?
2. Are you sensitive to sin?
3. Do you obey God's Word?
4. Do you reject this evil world?
5. Do you eagerly await Christ's return?
6. Do you see a decreasing pattern of sin in your life?
7. Do you love other Christians?
8. Do you experience answered prayer?
9. Do you experience the ministry of the Holy Spirit?

Admittedly, if these tests must be passed to have assurance, no one could have it.

For example, how could anyone know if he has enjoyed fellowship with God unless he was already certain he had a *relationship* with God? If you aren't sure on the basis of faith in Christ that you have eternal life, then you would always wonder if what you thought was fellowship was merely religious activity.

Sensitivity to sin could not result in assurance. The Holy Spirit convicts all people of sin (John 16:9-11). Lots of unbelievers are quite sensitive to their sins.

Besides, like the other elements on this list, sensitivity to sin is quite subjective. Who is to say that he is sensitive *enough?*

Obedience to God's Word is, according to John himself in 1 John 1:8, 10, imperfect. We all sin repeatedly, and will never reach the point in this life where we can honestly say, "I no longer sin." Thus whatever obedience we experience is relative and subjective. It cannot prove one is born again. At best, obedience can validate that we are walking in fellowship with God and are mature believers (and then only if we are already certain we are children of God), since fellowship with God includes the confession of sins (1 John 1:9).

The point is that every item on this list is subjective. And the problem isn't just with this particular list. *Any* list of tests based on First John is flawed if its purpose is seen as evaluating whether one is born again.

Now if we are talking about assurance of *fellowship* with God, this list makes sense. If we already know by faith alone that we are eternally secure (1 John 5:9-13), these subjective tests can show us that we are in fellowship with God at the present time.

Of course, since we might fall away in the future, we know that our fellowship may later be broken.

That is another problem with the *tests of life* view. If a person thought "I'm doing well in all these tests and hence I'm probably born again," he knows that could change. If he fell in the future, then he would prove that what he had thought was assurance of salvation was not really assurance. Or, equally bad, he would discover that he lost eternal life because he ceased passing the tests.

FELLOWSHIP IS RELATED TO OUR BEHAVIOR

While our *relationship* with God is not in any way dependent on our behavior, our *fellowship* is. The believer who does not confess the sins which the Holy Spirit reveals to him is not in fellowship with God (1 John 1:9). The believer who does not confess Christ is not in fellowship with God (1 John 2:22-23). If a believer does not meet the needs of believers in his church when those needs come to his attention, then he is not in fellowship with God (1 John 3:16-18).

Is not the same true in our earthly families?

When I grew up I always knew I was a member of the Wilkin family no matter what I did. I never feared being kicked out to live on the streets if I did something wrong or failed to do something I was supposed to do. But there was never any doubt that if I disobeyed my parents, our fellowship would be broken. I didn't like that experience. So I obeyed my parents as best I could, and confessed when I didn't, so as to remain in fellowship with them.

Children need the certain knowledge that they are secure in their earthly families. That certainty helps them live as they should and be in fellowship with their parents. The same is true in the family of God.

FELLOWSHIP, NOT ASSURANCE

There are two major views concerning *where* we find the purpose statement in First John.

Those who see First John as written to give the readers assurance of eternal life find the purpose of the letter in 5:13:

> These things I have written to you who believe in the name of the Son of God, that you may know that you have eternal life, and that you may continue to believe in the name of the Son of God.

Others consider that the book was written so that the readers might know that they were continuing to walk in fellowship with God. They contend the purpose statement is contained in 1:3-4:

> …that which we have seen and heard we declare to you, that you also may have fellowship with us; and truly our fellowship is with the Father and with His Son Jesus Christ. And these things we write to you that your joy may be full.

Let's first examine the *tests of life* view of First John. Those who hold this view suggest that the words, "These things I have written to you" at the beginning of 5:13 indicate that what follows is the purpose of *the entire letter*. That may sound convincing if you don't know the whole book. After all, John does say in 5:13 that assurance is the reason he has written *these things*. But to what does the expression *these things* refer?

The expression "these things I [or we] have written [or write] to you" occurs three other times in the book. In 2:1 John said, "*These things I write to you, so that you may not sin*" (italics added). No one thinks that 2:1 is the purpose statement of the whole letter. Clearly John is referring to what he had just written in 1:5-10.

In 1 John 2:26 John wrote, "*These things I have written to you concerning those who try to deceive you*" (italics added). Again, no one mistakes this for the purpose of the whole letter. John is referring to what he wrote in 2:24-25.

The same is true in 1 John 5:13. There "these things I have written to you" concerns 5:9-12, where, logically enough, John talks about assurance. In this paragraph, near the end of the letter, John talks about assurance because it is foundational to walking in fellowship with Christ.[2]

There remains one other use of this expression in First John. It is found in the opening verses of the book, which is where purpose statements for letters were normally found in that day.

John wrote, "*These things we write to you* that your joy may be full" (italics added). Note that this time John refers to what *we* write. In the other three examples John used the first person *singular*. Why the shift between first person plural in 1:3-4 and first person singular in the other three places? I believe John uses *we* in First John 1:3-4 to set it apart from the other three statements.

Additionally, in 1:3-4 John is emphasizing that he is speaking for the entire band of apostles.

Thus of the four times John uses the expression "these things I [or we] have written [or write] to you," three deal with the purpose of the immediate context only. The purpose of the whole letter was that John's readers might continue to walk in fellowship with God (1:3-4).

KEEPING HIS COMMANDMENTS (2:3-11)

"Now by this we know that we know Him, if we keep His commandments" (1 John 2:3). The word *know* is a flexible term. If we say, "He never really *knew* his wife," it is understood that there was a lack of intimacy in the relationship. Similarly, a person can be a child of God and yet not *know* God in his experience. Consider a new Christian. How could he know God in his experience, since according to John he must keep God's commandments to know Him? A brand new Christian has not had time to keep His commandments! He may not even be aware of what they are. He needs to grow to know God experientially.

Jesus made this point to the disciples in the upper room on the night He was betrayed. Speaking to Philip, the Lord said, "Have I been with you so long, and yet you have not *known* Me...?" (John 14:9, italics added). There was a sense in which the disciples didn't yet know Him. Of course, when He was crucified and they all lost faith, it was clear that their knowledge of Him was not yet what it should have been.

So, the point in 1 John 2:3-11 is that our knowledge of God is directly related to our holiness. It is probably fair to say that while all mature Christians know God (1 Corinthians 2:14), there is a sense in which we can grow to know Him better as we become more like Christ. The issue is not assurance of salvation, but how intimately we know God in our experience.

LOVING OUR BROTHERS (3:14)

The expression *has passed from death into life* is found in two places in the writings of John: John 5:24 and 1 John 3:14.

John 5:24 reads, "Most assuredly, I say to you, he who hears My word and believes in Him who sent Me has everlasting life, and shall not come into judgment, but has passed from death into life." The context of John 5:24 makes it clear that the phrase *has passed from death into life* there refers to *the position* of the one who believes in Jesus. That is because it is preceded by the words *has everlasting life* and *shall not come into judgment* [better, condemnation].

The context is completely different in 1 John 3:14. John is writing about the way in which a person's *experience* manifests what sort of person he is. First John 3:14 reads, "We know that we have passed from death to life, because we love the brethren. He who does not love his brother abides in death." A Christian lives like a child of God when he loves his fellow brothers and sisters. A Christian lives like a child of the devil when he hates his fellow brothers and sisters.

The way we know we've passed from the sphere of death to the sphere of life *in our experience* is because we love other Christians. Clearly that is different from the way we know we have positionally passed from death to life (John 5:24). We know that by faith alone.

The last sentence in 1 John 3:14 confirms the point: "He who does not love *his brother* abides in death" (italics added). Only a Christian is capable of not loving *his brother* in Christ. An unbeliever has no brother in Christ to love or not to love!

Note as well that the issue is where the believer abides. The believer who does not love his brother "abides [in the sphere of] death." Cain killed his brother Abel because he did not love him (Genesis 4:3-8, 1 John 3:11-12). Thus Cain was abiding in death.

The main idea of the passage is not whether Cain was born again. The point is that if we hate our brother, we are abiding in the sphere of death. Even if we don't actually kill our brother as Cain did, failure to love a Christian brother or sister means that we are out of fellowship with God and are not abiding in the sphere of life.

FIRST JOHN IS ABOUT FELLOWSHIP

Recognizing that the issue in First John is fellowship, not assurance, unlocks the epistle. We can be sure we have everlasting life. First John doesn't undermine certainty. Indeed, properly understood, it affirms that if we simply accept God's testimony, we *know* we have eternal life (5:9-13).

---

[1] John MacArthur, Jr., *Saved Without a Doubt: How to Be Sure of Your Salvation* (Wheaton, IL: Victor Books, 1992), pp. 67-91.

[2] See R. T. Kendall, *Once Saved, Always Saved* (Chicago: Moody Press, 1983), p. 74. He says, "As long as there is doubt about your eternal standing in God's grace, there will be an impediment to your having fellowship with the Father."

— Chapter 16 —

CAMOUFLAGE CHRISTIANS

Probably all of us have at one time or another had an opportunity to be a witness for Christ and failed to take it.

Worse still, many of us probably have on occasion done what the apostle Peter did. He denied Christ. Peter not only didn't testify to his faith in Jesus, he actually denied being one of His followers or even knowing Him at all!

We may not have denied Jesus that blatantly, but we may have hidden the fact that we are Christians and that is essentially the same thing.

The Gospel of John tells us that there were many early Jewish believers in Jesus Christ who hid the fact that they believed in Jesus. Since Jews who confessed Jesus as the Messiah were being kicked out of the synagogues, many suppressed the fact that they believed in Jesus. This was true even among the rulers of Israel.

This has bearing on assurance of salvation since many pastors and theologians today teach that all genuinely born-again people consistently confess Christ. They would argue that anyone who denies Christ, at least for long, proves that he is a false professor.

If you are convinced that all true believers confess Christ consistently, and if you find yourself being silent about your faith, you will surely have doubts about whether you are born again.

There are lots of great reasons to confess our faith in Christ. To keep us from worrying about hell, however, is not one of them. It is a misunderstanding of John's Gospel and other New Testament texts on confessing Christ that results in this assurance-destroying doctrine.

JOHN 2:23-25

The first of these secret disciple passages is found in John 2:23-24. John there reports:

> Now when He was in Jerusalem at the Passover, during the feast, many believed in His name when they saw the signs which He did. But Jesus did not commit Himself to them because He knew all men and had no need that anyone should testify of man, because He knew what was in man.

John says, "Many *believed in His name*" (italics added). In the prologue of his Gospel, John said that all who "believe in His name" are born of God (John 1:12-13). Thus these were people who failed to confess Jesus, but who were nonetheless born again.

Now, it is true that the same Greek word, *pisteuō*, translated *believe* in verse 23, is used in verse 24 in a different sense. John says of the new *believers* of verse 23, "Jesus *did not commit* Himself to them" (italics added). John is employing a simple play on words that any Greek reader of that day would have understood.

One of the rarer meanings of *pisteuō* is *to commit* in the sense of *to entrust*. For example, if I put money in a bank, I am committing or entrusting my money to it. Clearly that doesn't in any way suggest that I am promising to serve the bank. I am simply entrusting my money to the bank's safekeeping.

Jesus was not *entrusting* Himself to these new *believers*. Now we know from the Upper Room discourse that Jesus gave special instruction to the apostles because they were His friends and they were doing what He commanded. And so He manifested Himself to them in a special way (John 14:21; 15:15). What John 2:23-25 is saying is that Jesus was not *entrusting* these new *believers* with more truth since they were not worthy of more truth.

Why weren't they worthy of more truth? The reason, as we shall soon see, is they were afraid to confess their faith in Jesus.

But before we show that, it's vital to recognize that there is nothing in John 2:23-25 even remotely suggesting that confessing Christ is a condition of eternal life. We are born again if we believe what Jesus said, that all who believe in Him have everlasting life (e.g., John 6:47). It is possible to believe that and yet fail to confess Jesus. The apostle Peter, for example, believed in Jesus when he denied Him three times.

John 2:23-27 ends with a cryptic explanation why Jesus didn't entrust Himself to these new believers: "[He] had no need that anyone should testify of man, for He knew what was in *man*" (italics added). John 3:1 begins, "There was a *man* named Nicodemus" (italics added). There's a clear connection with the repetition of the word *man*. Nicodemus illustrates the problem Jesus had with these new believers.

Nicodemus is the prime example in John's Gospel of the secret believer. In each of the three times he is mentioned in John's

Gospel, John tells us that he "came to Jesus by night" (3:2; 7:50; 19:39). Why? Because Nicodemus didn't want anyone to know that he was interested in Jesus. In chapter 7 John records that Nicodemus hid the fact that he believed in Jesus from his fellow Jewish leaders. John tells us in chapter 19 that Nicodemus came with Joseph of Arimathea to claim the body of Jesus, stating plainly that Joseph was "a disciple of Jesus, but secretly, for fear of the Jews." Clearly since John says that Nicodemus came with Joseph, he is implying that Nicodemus too was a secret follower of Jesus.

I believe Nicodemus came to faith in John 3 as Jesus evangelized him. But Jesus didn't entrust Himself to Nicodemus for he wasn't yet willing to confess Him before men. Therefore, in the story of Nicodemus we learn why Jesus didn't entrust Himself to the new believers of John 2. They too weren't yet willing to confess Him.

Keep in mind that the fact that Jesus didn't entrust further knowledge to a group of people says nothing about whether or not they were saved. It merely indicates that they were not yet worthy to receive more information from the Lord Jesus.

We find this same truth discussed elsewhere in John's Gospel. John 12:42-43 is a key passage in John concerning the secret believer motif.

JOHN 12:42-43

Nicodemus and Joseph of Arimathea were not the only rulers of Israel who secretly believed in Jesus. Actually, *many* of the leaders were camoflauge believers:

> Nevertheless even among the rulers many believed in Him, but because of the Pharisees they did not confess Him, lest they should be put out of the synagogue; for they loved the praise of men more than the praise of God.

Of course, some say that these rulers were false professors because they did not confess Jesus Christ and because they loved the praise of men more than the praise of God. This would suggest that all *true* believers *do* confess Christ and *do* prefer God's praise to men's. Matthew 10:32-33 is often cited as a proof text using Jesus' own words:

> Therefore whoever confesses Me before men, him will I also confess before My Father who is in heaven. But whoever denies Me before men, him will I also deny before My Father who is in heaven.

If only those who will be confessed by Christ are regenerate, the case is crystal clear. But, as is often the case, how one evaluates the facts makes all the difference.

The idea that these rulers were false professors is impossible unless John was mistaken. For it is John, not the rulers themselves, who said, "Nevertheless, even among the rulers many believed in Him." John, writing under inspiration, says that they believed in Jesus. Thus they did.

Still people do argue that this belief was less than saving. The problem with such a suggestion is that it flies in the face of John's other uses of the expression *believing in Him*. That expression is John's favorite way of referring to those who have eternal life. Remember the Lord's words to Nicodemus in John 3:16, "whoever *believes in Him* should not perish, but have everlasting life" (italics added). *Whoever* means whoever. The divine author of

Scripture, the Holy Spirit, didn't allow John to forget in chapter 12 what he had written in chapter 3. Therefore, we can only conclude that many of the rulers had everlasting life. So, if the text goes on to say that these believing rulers weren't confessing Christ, then the only conclusion we can draw is that it's possible for genuine believers not to confess Christ.

That's what the text says. They believed in Him, but they weren't confessing Him. Therefore, believers sometimes don't confess. And it goes on to say they loved the praise of men more than the praise of God. John is saying it's possible for a believer to love the praise of men more than the praise of God. And we find examples of that all through the Scriptures.

It's naive to think that Christians never love the praise of men more than the praise of God. And it's naive to think that Christians always confess Christ in word and deed.

As mentioned earlier, John specifically tells us in chapter 19 of two of the rulers, Joseph and Nicodemus, who came out in the open a bit when they claimed the body of Jesus for burial. While that wasn't an open profession of faith in Christ, it must have angered the rulers of Israel who didn't believe in Jesus. Surely they wanted Jesus buried in a pauper's grave next to the two thieves.

Matthew 10:32-33 is not stating some additional condition of regeneration besides faith in Christ. If it were, then justification wouldn't be by faith alone. It would be by faith plus confession of Christ.

When Jesus says, "He who confesses me before men, him will I also confess before my Father who is in heaven," He's talking about the Judgment Seat of Christ. And that's brought out in 2 Timothy 2:12-13, where Paul picks up on verse 33 and says, "If we endure, we shall also reign with Him. If we deny Him, He will also deny us. If we are faithless, He remains faithful; He cannot deny Himself." If we deny Christ, He's going to deny us the privilege of ruling with Him. Only believers who endure in their confession of Christ will reign. Yet He must remain faithful to His promise that whoever believes in Him has everlasting life. Not all Christians will be confessed by Christ before the Father as those who will rule in the life to come.

So what happens if a Christian confesses Christ for years, and then becomes like the believing members of the Sanhedrin and stops confessing Christ? Some would say that all that's required is a one-time confession of Christ. Yet 2 Timothy 2:12 makes it clear that we must *endure* in our confession of Christ until death or the rapture. We need to live each day as though it might be our last. Our lives are like vapors, and they indeed could end at any moment. If we are secret believers when we die, we will miss out forever on ruling with Christ—even if we confessed Him faithfully for decades. However, we will not miss out on the kingdom, for the only condition of eternal life and kingdom entrance is believing in Jesus.

Confessing Christ

Assurance of salvation does not depend on confessing one's faith in Christ. Jesus guarantees eternal life to all who simply believe in Him.

The secret disciple motif in John's Gospel does not undermine assurance. In fact, it is based upon it.

Those who know themselves to be eternally secure simply by faith in Jesus may choose to be silent about their faith. But that is a foolish thing to do. For, as John implies in John 12:43, if you did that, you would ultimately miss out on God's praise at the Judgment Seat of Christ. Plus you would experience God's discipline now, rather than His hand of blessing.

By all means, be an open follower of Jesus Christ. Indeed, I hope we will all go beyond merely confessing that we are followers of Christ. Hopefully we will regularly seize the opportunity to tell others that if they simply believe in Jesus they will be eternally secure. It's a privilege to tell people that wonderful news.

Most in America have heard and believe that Jesus died on the cross and rose again from the dead. But they haven't heard that a person is born again *once and for all.* Eternal security is something many have never heard. Nor have most heard that the sole condition of eternal life is simple faith in Jesus, the One who died and rose again. What a joy it is to share that message.

So, don't be a camouflage Christian. Stand out for Jesus Christ. People may take pot shots at you. That's fine. It's a privilege to suffer persecution for the King of kings.

If we confess Him now, then He will confess us at the Judgment Seat of Christ. And if He confesses us at that time, then we will rule with Him forever. While all believers are eternally secure, only some will rule with Christ. Make it your aim in life to be part of that privileged group.

— Chapter 17 —

YOU WILL KNOW THEM
BY THEIR FRUITS

What role does fruit play in assurance? Do you look at your life and see how fruitful you are for Christ in order to decide if you have "the right stuff"?

If so, what do you do when you see sinful attitudes and actions in your life?

And if you do begin to doubt that you're born again, there really is very little you can do to remove those doubts, especially for those who have deep-seated problems in their lives.

The teaching that fruit is an indispensable means of having assurance is not one that works well among people suffering from depression, worry, guilt, anxiety, stress, discouragement, perfectionism, obsessive-compulsive disorder, or a host of other emotional problems. Indeed, I've found that such a teaching disables those who are hurting inside. I'm not suggesting that it works well for those not suffering from emotional problems. After all, to some degree we all struggle with our emotions. But this view is especially hurtful to the most sensitive among us.[1]

Now this doesn't make the doctrine wrong. However, if we find that a doctrine doesn't work practically, we surely should go back to the Scriptures to see if we are reading them correctly.

There are two main proof texts for this idea. Let's first consider the famous statement from the Sermon on the Mount: "By their fruits you will know them" (Matthew 7:16, 20).

By Their Fruits

I am asked about this saying often when I speak around the country. Most people think Jesus is talking about how we identify born-again people.

Actually the people Jesus is talking about are not believers, but false prophets! Note Matthew 7:15-16:

> Beware of false prophets, who come to you in sheep's clothing, but inwardly they are ravenous wolves. *You will know them by their fruits.* Do men gather grapes from thornbushes or figs from this-tles? (italics added).

False prophets "come to you in sheep's clothing, but inwardly they are ravenous wolves." They look good on the outside, but looks can be deceiving.

The fruits of the false prophets are their *words*, their *teachings*. That is how you identify a false prophet or a false teacher. This is confirmed by a passage later in Matthew where Jesus, again talk-ing about fruit (Matthew 12:33, "a tree is known by its fruits"), says "For out of the abundance of the heart the mouth speaks" (Matthew 12:34).

Matthew 7:15-20 ends with a repetition of the statement "by their fruits you will know them." This is then followed in verses 21-23 with an account of how false prophets and others will try to defend themselves at the Great White Throne Judgment. Yet these people will not get into the kingdom, for they never believed in Jesus.

By their fruits you will know them is never used in the Bible in reference to believers. It is used only of unbelievers. This supposed "proof" is no proof at all.

The second proof text for this idea is found in The Parable of the Four Soils (Luke 8:5-15).

WHO BEARS MUCH FRUIT?

If only the fourth soil (Luke 8:8, 15) represents born-again people, then all born-again people are good soil and all produce mature fruit.

The entire parable is thus viewed in this way:

Soil one represents the out-and-out unbeliever who doesn't go to church and doesn't profess faith in Christ (Luke 8:5, 12).

The second soil represents the unbeliever who for a time goes to church and professes Christ and even does good works. But after a short time his true colors appear, he stops believing in Jesus (Luke 8:13), and he proves that he was a false professor all along.

Soil three represents the unbeliever who for his whole life goes to church, professes faith in Christ, and does good works. But his works never come up to the measure of what we call *mature fruit* (Luke 8:14). This person proves to be a false professor because his works show that he is halfhearted in his service for Christ. He doesn't maximize his life for Christ. Thus over the course of years or decades, it becomes evident to the discerning viewer that this person probably never was born again in the first place.

The fourth soil represents the believer who for his whole Christian life goes to church, professes faith in Christ, and does good works. Unlike the first three soils, this type of believer is wholehearted in his service for Christ and produces mature fruit (Luke 8:15). He proves that he is a true professor because his works give real evidence of the new birth.

While that is a common way of understanding the parable, it doesn't fit the particulars well at all.

SPRINGING UP

Nearly all commentators agree that one or more of the soils represent believers, and one or more unbelievers. The question is, what in the parable indicates which soils represent believers and which unbelievers?

A commonly cited indicator is fruit bearing. Only soil four bears mature fruit. Thus in this view, only soil four represents believers.

In this way of looking at the parable, Jesus is telling us about three different types of *unbelievers*. He wants us to realize that not all who believe the good news are born again. Those who only believe for a time and then fall away prove they were never really born again. Those who believe the good news their whole life, but fail to wholeheartedly serve Christ and fail to develop mature fruit also prove they were never born again.

However, another indicator screams out of the text as being the correct determiner of who is born again and who is not. That is germination of the seed.

The seed in the first soil did not germinate. Life didn't begin.

The seed in the second, third, and fourth soils all "sprang up." In Luke 8:6-8, Jesus explains,

> "Some fell on the rock; and as soon as it *sprang up*, it withered away because it lacked moisture. And some fell among thorns, and the thorns *sprang up with it* and choked it. But others fell on good ground, *sprang up*, and yielded a crop a hundred-fold." When He [Jesus] had said these things He cried, "He who has ears to hear, let him hear!" (italics added).

Obviously if a plant breaks the surface of the ground, the seed below ground has already germinated. It is physically impossible for a plant to spring up without life having begun.[2]

Thus Jesus is telling us about three different types of *believers*.

Note that this is supported by the fact that Jesus specifically said that the second soil believed. He didn't say that such people *professed* faith. He said they *believed*. And it is clear, based on the references to unbelief in verse 12 and then belief in verse 13, that the message they believed was the saving message not believed by the first soil.

Beware: Some Believers Fall Away

The believer typified by the second soil fails to persevere in faith and good works. Jesus specifically says they "believe for a while and in time of temptation fall away." Jesus doesn't say how long they believe. Why? Because believers who fall away don't do so at any set point in their Christian lives. Some might fall away right after they come to faith in Christ. Others might fall away after years or decades of being a Christian.

Anyone who has been in ministry very long has seen many examples of this type of believer. To suggest that such people were never believers in the first place is directly contradicted by Jesus Himself. In the first place, He says the seed "sprang up." In the second place, He said these people believed for a time.

Clearly this is a warning: Beware, Christian, your faith may fail.[3] If anyone thinks he is impervious to the attacks of the world, the flesh, and the devil, he is much more likely to fall.

Beware: Some Believers Persevere in Mediocrity

There is a clear progression in the four soils from worst to best. Thus when we compare the third soil with the second and fourth soils, we get a good picture of what it is like in contrast with the other two.

Jesus doesn't say of the third soil, as He does of the second soil, that it "believed for a time." This shows that it represents believers whose faith persevered to the end. Whereas the second soil represents believers who "fall away" (Luke 8:13), the third soil represents believers who don't fall away.

Concerning fruit bearing, Jesus says that the seeds which fell among the thorns "bring no fruit to maturity" (Luke 8:14). Note that He doesn't say that these seeds "bring *no* fruit." There is a difference between bearing no fruit and bearing no *mature* fruit.

If you've ever had fruit trees, you know that if they are very distressed, they will put out leaves, but no fruit at all. If they are mildly distressed, they will put out leaves and fruit, however, the fruit will not develop fully. I remember a peach tree we had in California when I was a boy. Year after year it bore green hard peaches that never reached maturity. Maybe this was because we didn't water enough or because we didn't treat for bugs. Whatever the reason, my Dad and I looked disappointedly each year at that peach tree. It was like the third soil type of believer.

Jesus indicates why the fruit fails to come to maturity in the third soil. This type of believer is bogged down by "cares, riches, and the pleasures of life." He serves halfheartedly due to distractions (weeds).

Have you ever considered that cares in your life can hinder your service for Christ? This is why Peter tells us to cast all our cares upon Him (1 Peter 5:7). Surely you don't conclude if you are weighed down by cares that you are an unbeliever. What you conclude is that you are being hindered in your life and service.

But what about riches? We don't tend to think of riches as dangerous to our spiritual health. But they are. Riches can hinder our effectiveness just like cares can. The fact some believers are rich doesn't prove they are halfhearted in their service for Christ. But it means that they will have to battle that tendency more than believers who aren't rich.

And what about pleasures of life? Have you noticed that pleasures can hinder your effectiveness for Christ? Golf is fun, but if you are obsessed by golf, it could hinder your ability to serve God. The same is true with fishing, hunting, skiing, or any other hobby or pleasure we might have in life. Too much pleasure chokes our spiritual effectiveness like weeds choke plants.

Behold: Some Believers Persevere in Excellence

A believer who perseveres in faith and in wholehearted service for Christ is exemplified by the fourth soil. His productivity is not choked out by cares, riches, or pleasurable pursuits.

This type of person has "a noble and good heart" (Luke 8:15). But what does the heart have to do with anything?

The Bible is clear that our spiritual effectiveness is directly related to our intake of the Word of God. In Romans 12 Paul commands us to be transformed by the renewing of our minds. When He was tempted by Satan, the Lord said, "Man shall not live by bread alone, but by every word that proceeds from the mouth of God" (Matthew 4:4).

Indeed, immediately after this parable Jesus said, "Therefore take heed how you hear..." (Luke 8:18). The key to being the good soil type of believer is hearing the Word of God.

Do you want to be a believer who hears Christ's "Well done, good servant"? If you do, take heed how you hear the Word of God. Develop what Jesus calls "a noble and good heart." For the key to success in the Christian life is in God changing us from the inside out via the power of His life-transforming Word.

Losing Your Assurance

Now consider for a moment the impact of this passage on assurance if you are convinced that only the last type of believer gets into the kingdom.

If you found yourself weighed down by cares, you would conclude that you probably aren't truly saved.

If you found yourself thinking a lot about your finances, then you would doubt you were born again. And you would try to figure out how to get saved properly since whatever you did the first time didn't take.

And if you felt that you were not wholehearted in your service for Christ because of pleasurable pursuits like golf, tennis, television, movies, sports, and the like, then you would doubt you were the good soil and thus would figure you needed to really be born again this time.

Mark this well. No one can be certain he has eternal life if only those who are the good soil have eternal life.

In the first place it's hard to be certain that we fall in the category of the good soil. It would seem presumptuous, would it not, to say you are certain that God views you as the good soil? How do you know that you aren't the third soil, halfhearted in your service?

In the second place, even if you had good reason to believe you were good soil *now*, you could not be sure you would *remain* that way. If you later fell off in your productivity, it would prove that you were actually the weed-infested soil. Or if you stopped believing altogether, you would prove to be the rocky soil.

God doesn't want you to go through life trying to figure out if you have enough works to get into the kingdom and to prove you are His child. He wants you to be certain you have eternal life solely because you believe in the One who died for you and what He has promised: everlasting life to all who simply believe in Him.

God *does* want us to be concerned about our productivity so that we can please Him and gain the privilege of being Christ's coheirs. But that presupposes we are certain we have eternal life. Otherwise we end up doing good works in an effort to make it into the kingdom. That is legalism. That is justification by faith plus works.

The Parable of the Four Soils does not teach assurance by works. It teaches that we should strive to be wholehearted in our devotion for Christ. But it also shows that all those who simply believe in Jesus have everlasting life, with no works required to gain or maintain it.

LOOK TO YOUR FRUIT

We don't identify Christians by how much fruit they produce. We identify *how productive* Christians are by how much fruit they produce. There is a big difference between the two.

Let's say you had three fig trees in your yard and only one was producing good mature figs. You'd check things that hinder fruit production like hydration, exposure to the sun, fertilization, pest control, weed control, and the like. You know a tree will only produce mature fruit if it is properly nourished and if it is protected from weeds and pests.

That's the way we are in the Christian life. If you are fruitful in your service for Christ, great. Keep on taking heed how you hear the Word of God.

If you are halfhearted in your service for Christ, pay more attention to God's Word. You need more nourishment from God to be fully effective in your service. You may need to give up some of your hobbies. You may need to spend less time working on your investments. You may need to give more of your money away.

If you find doubts are creeping into your Christian life, get help from someone who is well grounded in the Word. Higher education can destroy the faith of Christians if they aren't careful. So can friends who are skeptics, the secular media, and even the cults.

Don't look to your fruit to see if you are born again. Look to your Savior for that. But look to your fruit to see how you are doing in your service for Christ.

---

[1] For a fascinating discussion of this issue by a leading Christian psychiatrist, see Frank B. Minirth, "The Psychological Effects of Lordship Salvation," *Journal of the Grace Evangelical Society* (Autumn 1993): pp. 39-51.

² Does this mean that every born-again person "springs up" in the sense of doing some good works? Yes, I believe it does. Except for those who die at the moment of the new birth, some changes occur in every believer that are capable of observation. However, we must be careful to avoid two erroneous applications of this truth. First, we may not be infallible observers. Thus we may not see the changes in a person. Even the person himself may not identify them. Second, these changes are not the basis of assurance. Assurance is found in believing in Jesus. That is objective. Our works are subjective and variable, as the parable clearly illustrates.

³ See Chapter 14, "Fractured Faith." Remember that even if a believer later stops believing, he remains eternally secure. He can lose joy and reward, but not eternal life. "Shall never die" is what Jesus promises (John 11:26). Never means never.

— Chapter 18 —

FACT OR FEELING?

During my four years in campus evangelism with Campus Crusade for Christ, we used a booklet, *The Four-Spiritual Laws*, that contained a discussion of assurance. The booklet included a discussion of the role of feelings in assurance. It did so using the illustration of a train with an engine, labeled *Fact*, and two cars, labeled *Faith* and *Feeling*.

The three-car train diagram illustrates that assurance comes when we have faith in the facts of the gospel found in God's Word. As long as our faith is in the facts of the promise of eternal life, we remain sure we have eternal life. The caboose (Feeling) in the illustration, neither drives the train nor is it directly attached to the engine. Feelings naturally follow faith in the facts. But feelings are never the basis of assurance. Feelings fluctuate. Facts do not.

However, there is a popular teaching today that born-again people possess a special feeling that assures them they are children of God.

First let's consider the Scripture used to support this idea. Then we will consider practical concerns.

THE SPIRIT BEARS WITNESS WITH OUR SPIRIT

Romans 8:16 says, "The Spirit Himself bears witness with our spirit that we are children of God."

Two Witnesses Give Legal Proof

Romans 8:16 does not say, "The Spirit Himself bears witness *to* our spirit that we are children of God." Actually the text says that He "bears witness *with* our spirit..." (italics added).

Paul is speaking of two witnesses, the Holy Spirit and our human spirit. They both bear witness *together*. This is in keeping with the Old Testament principle that all matters need to be verified by at least two witnesses.

The Holy Spirit and our human spirit both bear witness that we are children of God. But to whom is this witness directed?

They Witness to the Father, Not to Us

Romans 8:15 indicates that when we pray we cry out, "Abba, Father." This suggests that the Person to whom our human spirit "bears witness" is also God the Father. If the Spirit is bearing witness *with* our human spirit, then He, too, bears witness to God the Father. Romans 8:26 confirms this conclusion, asserting that whenever we pray the Holy Spirit intercedes for us. Clearly the Person to whom He is interceding is God the Father.

The dual witness occurs whenever we pray. That is when our human spirit cries out to God the Father. Simultaneously the

Holy Spirit witnesses to God the Father that we are indeed His children.

Of course, we cannot feel, see, hear, or in any way tune into this witness of the Holy Spirit to God the Father—even though in our experience of prayer we might have a general sense that the Holy Spirit is at work. The only sure way we know He does this is because the Bible tells us He does.

Romans 8:16 Isn't an Assurance Verse

Romans 8:16 is a statement about what happens as we pray. It is encouraging to know that as we pray the Holy Spirit is echoing the sentiment of our inner selves: *this one is a child of God.*

There is no biblical support for looking to our feelings to gain assurance that we have eternal life.

If we accept the testimony of God the Father concerning His Son, then we *know* we have eternal life (1 John 5:9-13). Assurance is objective. It is sourced in the gospel.

GOD'S WORD ABIDES FOREVER

Do you look to your feelings to know if you are an American citizen? Of course not. Feelings have nothing to do with it. Your birth certificate proves your citizenship.

The birth certificate of the believer is God's Word. It objectively testifies to us that all who believe in Jesus are citizens of heaven.

Feelings only inform us about our feelings!

If I'm angry with my parents, that doesn't mean I'm not their child. And if I'm angry with God, that doesn't mean I'm not one of His children.

Conversely, if I feel great affection for a couple old enough to be my parents, that doesn't prove I'm their child. And if I have loving feelings toward God, that doesn't mean I'm His child.

If we based our assurance on feelings, then we could be misled in either direction. Unbelievers might be convinced they were born again because they felt a special love for Jesus. Believers might be convinced they were not born again because they no longer had the deep love for Christ they once had.

God's Word abides forever. It is stable, dependable. It never changes. You can believe what it says. And when you do, then you know that to be true.

The train diagram mentioned earlier warns that feelings come and go. It cautions against placing any confidence in our feelings. Assurance is based on believing the facts, not on looking at our feelings.

That is great advice. Assurance is fact-based, not feeling-based. Those who search for some special feeling do so in vain because God does not promise us any special feeling. We walk by faith, not by sight, and not by feelings. The Scriptures are the eternal witness of the Holy Spirit to us. They testify that all who simply believe in Jesus have everlasting life. That's good news.

~ Section 4 ~

ANSWERING OBJECTIONS

*Always be ready to give a defense
to everyone who asks you a reason
for the hope that is in you.*
1 Peter 3:15

— Chapter 19 —

WHY IS CERTAINTY SO OBJECTIONABLE?

This question has puzzled me for a long time. Many Christian leaders in a wide variety of churches and denominations are adamantly opposed to certainty. I've debated quite a few who were downright hostile toward the idea that we can be certain we are eternally secure no matter what we might do in the future.

In the chapters which follow, we'll consider biblical objections by Christian leaders. However, in this chapter, which serves as an introduction to this section of the book, we'll consider the underlying concerns that lead to those objections. People sometimes come up with interpretations due to theological systems that they have adopted and which they then unwittingly impose upon passages of Scripture.

Many theological traditions raise philosophical and practical objections to certainty.

It Seems to Promote Ungodliness

Many think that fear of hell is necessary to keep people away from ungodliness. Remove that fear and people would be set free to a life of immorality.

This is obviously the thinking of those who believe that eternal life can be lost through sin.

However, it is also the belief of many who hold to eternal security. Many Calvinists are convinced that perseverance in good works is needed to prove who is eternally secure. Thus all professing believers are to fear hell since if they fail to persevere, they will prove they never truly believed in the first place.

My reply to this objection is simple. Certainty of eternal security promotes godliness, not ungodliness.

While a person who knows himself to be eternally secure might abuse grace, that is not in any way to say that grace promotes sin. The person who is certain of God's love is far more likely to live a God-pleasing life than the one who is not.

Don't we see this in our human families?

A child who grows up in a home where the love of his parents is in doubt is far more likely to become a hostile, insecure, and dysfunctional adult. But the child who grows up in a home where he is certain of the love of his mother and father is much more likely to become a loving, secure, and highly productive adult.

If good human parents want their children to be secure in the knowledge that they are part of the family no matter what, why would our heavenly Father want less for His children?

Having a secure childhood doesn't guarantee success in life. But it makes it much more likely.

IT SEEMS TO DESTROY THE MAIN
MOTIVATION TO LIVE FOR GOD

A closely related objection concerns our motivation to serve God. Many feel that a healthy fear of hell is one of the most important motivations for Christians to live for God.

Most would agree that there are other motivations to live for God including the love of God, a sense of duty, fear of His discipline, and a desire for well being. However, those motivations receive little attention in Christian preaching and writings today. Many preachers and authors view all other motivations combined to be of lesser importance than fear of hell.

Christian leaders might illustrate this concern with the example of a person who is financially set for life. A person who has a trust fund that guarantees him and his family a good living for life may be motivated by reasons other than financial concerns to get a job and be productive. However, he is likely to be far less motivated than a person who knows that if he doesn't work, he and his family will be homeless and destitute.

My reply is that fear of hell should motivate the *unbeliever* to seek out what he needs to do to have eternal life. Then, once he hears and believes the good news, he knows he is eternally secure, and that fear should be gone forever.

The one who is certain is not like a person whose financial concerns are guaranteed in this life. He's like a person whose basic needs are assured *in the life to come*. There's a big difference.

One who is eternally secure and who fails to live for God may be depressed, sick, financially destitute, disheartened, and possibly even homeless. The believer who doesn't live for God is miserable, even if he has lots of money and possessions. Only by living for God can a person have well being, peace of mind, and fulfillment.

Of course, all believers will have well being in the life to come. But some will have more abundant lives than others. So whether we are speaking of this life or the one to come, obeying God is always in our best interest (1 Timothy 4:8).

It Seems to Garble the Gospel

If God wants to keep His children in doubt about their eternal destiny until they die, then anyone who shares the message of certainty is distorting the saving message.

Nearly all who deny certainty say that more than simple faith in Jesus is required in order for a person to have eternal life. They may suggest that commitment of life is part of saving faith. Turning from sins may be mentioned as a condition. So might obedience. Or baptism.

At the very least all who reject certainty believe that perseverance in faith and good works is necessary for a person to make it into the kingdom. Those who fail to persevere won't make it.

My response is that while this may seem reasonable, it is not the gospel of Jesus and His apostles. Evangelism, as the Lord and His apostles practiced it, involves sharing the message of certainty, not suppressing it.

As I've shown many times in this book, Jesus and his apostles promised eternal life to all who simply believe in Him. They didn't state any other conditions. The reason theologians coined the expression *justification by faith alone* is because the only condition stated in the Bible for justification before God is faith in Jesus Christ.

Actually it is those who fail to teach certainty who are guilty of flawed evangelism. For certainty of eternal life is the promise of the gospel. If we don't tell a person that Jesus guarantees eternal life to the one who simply believes in Him, then we haven't told them the promise of the gospel.

CERTAINTY ISN'T THE HISTORIC TEACHING OF CHRISTIANITY

Christian scholars point out that the prevailing view in the history of the church has always been that certainty is impossible. The church fathers didn't believe certainty was possible. Neither did Augustine. The Puritans, the English branch of the Reformation, denied the possibility of certainty as well.

I concede this point. It is true that the prevailing view has always been uncertainty. Oh, there have been people who have believed in and promoted certainty. But they were always in the minority.[1]

My reply to this objection is simple. Truth is found in the Bible, not in tradition.

That's why I've not tried to prove, for example, that Calvin and Luther believed in certainty. What difference would that make one way or the other? The issue is what the Bible teaches.

Admittedly, the vast majority of pastors and theologians in church history believed in justification by faith plus works. Thus, most believed no one could be sure of his eternal destiny until he died. But most were wrong.

Jesus said that the way is narrow that leads to life and *few* find it (Matthew 7:14). It should come as no surprise that few in church history believed in certainty.

In my youth I was strongly influenced by a group that denied the possibility of certainty about as strongly as any group could. So I know how hard it is to embrace certainty when it conflicts with your tradition. However, when I did grasp certainty, I experienced joy and gratitude. Not only that, I found that certainty unlocked the Scriptures. Other doctrines like eternal rewards and temporal discipline emerged for me.

Certainty is true even if it conflicts with the historic position of most branches of Christianity.

CERTAINTY NEED NOT BE OBJECTIONABLE

If after reading this far in the book you are still battling with uncertainty, I hope you will abandon the philosophical and theological objections I've mentioned in this chapter. They simply do not hold up under careful scrutiny. And once you let go of these hindrances, you are much more likely to see and believe the truth of certainty.

Admittedly, the word *sure* has four letters in it. But that doesn't make it a Christian curse word. Certainty need not be objectionable. Indeed, it shouldn't be, for it is what God teaches us in His Word. God wants His children to be sure. Does it really make sense to you that He'd want anything less for you?

---

[1] For examples of people who believed in certainty, see Michael Makidon, "From Perth to Pennsylvania: The Legacy of Robert Sandeman" and "The Marrow Controversy," *Journal of the Grace Evangelical Society* (Spring 2002 and Autumn 2003): pp. 75-92 and 65-77. Both are available at www.faithalone.org. See also Thomas G. Lewellen, "Has Lordship Salvation Been Taught throughout Church History?" *Bibliotheca Sacra* (January 1990): pp. 54-68.

— Chapter 20 —

ONLY GOD KNOWS

Walter Chantry's very popular little book, *Today's Gospel: Authentic or Synthetic?* analyzes the gospel in light of Jesus' encounter with the rich young ruler. In a chapter on assurance, Chantry argues that no one can be sure he himself is born again for only God knows for sure.

JESUS' EVANGELISM DIDN'T INCLUDE ASSURANCE

Chantry begins by decrying the evangelistic approach of linking assurance with God's promises:

> So many Christian workers feel compelled to do the Holy Spirit's work of giving assurance in their evangelism…A sentence is added to the "salvation liturgy" which is not so much addressed to God as to the sinner who is repeating the prayer. "Thank

you for coming into my life and for hearing my prayer as you promised." Then the personal worker is to open his Bible to John 3:16 etc., and replace the word "world" with the sinner's name. Then the misguided counselor is to assure the sinner with all the authority of God that he has been saved. A warning is added not to sin against God by ever doubting his salvation, for that would be to call God a liar.[1]

Chantry bases his charge that assurance is not part of the gospel on Jesus' encounter with the rich young ruler. Since Jesus did not offer him assurance, Chantry evidently feels justified in saying that Jesus didn't offer anyone assurance and neither should we.

But is that a reasonable conclusion? As we look at passages like Luke 10:20 or John 6:35-40 or John 11:25-27, it is clear Jesus offered certainty of eternal life on many occasions.

Chantry's whole premise that Jesus' encounter with the rich young ruler is a fully developed evangelistic presentation is highly questionable. Jesus didn't explicitly call the rich young ruler to faith in Him and He never mentioned eternal life.[2] This encounter was *pre-evangelism*. Jesus was showing the rich young ruler his need of eternal life without telling him what he must do to get it. Clearly no one is justified by keeping the law (Luke 18:9-14; Romans 3:20; Galatians 2:15-16; 3:6-14).[3]

Of course, there is no prayer that someone needs to pray to be born again. Chantry is right in that regard. But that issue is completely unrelated to certainty.

A CALL TO BOW TO HIS RULE

Dr. Chantry is deeply grieved by what he considers to be counterfeit evangelism. True evangelism always calls the listener to repent, bow to Christ's rule, and bear one's cross:

> This heretical and soul-destroying practice is the logical conclusion of a system that thinks little of God, preaches no law, calls for no repentance, waters down faith to "accepting a gift," and never mentions bowing to Christ's rule or bearing a cross. The very practice of trying to argue men into assurance with a verse or two, and the ridiculous warning, "Don't call God a liar" shows that even "accepting the gift" requires only an outward response and a verbal prayer...[4]

Frankly, this is confusing. Clearly he believes saving faith is not merely being convinced that Jesus guarantees eternal life to the one who believes in Him. True faith includes "bowing to Christ's rule or bearing a cross." But how does that prove one can't be certain? Under that way of thinking, if a person fulfills those conditions, wouldn't he be sure?

Yes, he would be sure, but only if he were sure he had fulfilled the conditions; and Chantry admits that's impossible. No one can be sure he has eternal life if those are the conditions. Chantry has assumed we understand that all of the conditions he mentioned are subjective in nature. One cannot be sure he has sufficiently bowed to Christ's rule, taken up his cross, repented, and understood and obeyed the law. Besides, everyone knows he might slip in the future. And future failure in any of these areas would prove that one didn't really fulfill those conditions in the first place. In

Chantry's way of looking at the gospel, one must persevere to the end of his life in repentance, obedience, submission, and suffering.

HAVE WE DONE ENOUGH?

In light of his understanding of Jesus' encounter with the rich young ruler, Chantry goes on to suggest that Jesus wants us to doubt whether we've done enough. It is right, he believes, to have self doubt and hence for him certainty is impossible. Chantry says:

> Few today seem to understand the Bible's doctrine of assurance. Few seem to appreciate the doubts of professing Christians who question whether they have been born again. They have no doubt that God will keep His promises *but they wonder whether they have properly fulfilled the conditions* for being heirs to those promises.[5]

Chantry affirms here what he implied earlier. There are conditions (plural) of gaining eternal life: "They wonder whether they have properly fulfilled the conditions for being heirs of those promises." The problem does not lie with God in fulfilling His promises, but in us doing our part.

VALID QUESTIONS

Chantry continues:

> There is no question that God will give eternal life to all who repent and believe. But they are discerning enough to know that walking an aisle and muttering a verbal prayer does not constitute faith. The [Westminster] Catechism's doctrine has raised valid questions concerning their personal

experience of grace which cannot be brushed aside. They are asking a legitimate question, "Have we believed and repented?" "Are we the recipients of God's grace?"[6]

While I certainly agree that walking an aisle and praying a prayer are not faith, Chantry's argument is a bit of a straw man. It's possible to proclaim justification by faith alone without mentioning aisle walking or praying a sinner's prayer. The real issue is that for Chantry there are *conditions*, plural. For him believing the facts of the gospel is not enough. One must also repent, commit, and persevere in obedience.

Chantry indicates that "the Catechism's doctrine has raised valid questions concerning their personal experience of grace." Why Chantry mentions the Catechism at all is puzzling. Surely he believes it is Scripture and not a man-made confession that determines what we should believe.

Evidently Chantry believes that the Westminster Catechism accurately reflects what the Bible teaches. Hence, for him, reading the Catechism is on par with reading Scripture. But that is not correct, as this very discussion shows. The Bible teaches certainty. The Westminster Catechism does not.

ONLY GOD KNOWS FOR SURE

The final proof cited by Chantry that we can't be sure relates to Judas:

> Are we recipients of God's grace? Since we read of self-deceived hypocrites like Judas, it is an imperative question. "What must I do to be saved?" is an altogether different question from, "How do I know I've done it?" You can answer

the first confidently. Only the Spirit may
answer the last with certainty.[7]

Nowhere in the Bible are we told that Judas was "self-deceived." We never read that he believed in Jesus or that he thought he believed in Him.

But the most important point to notice here is Chantry's claim that we can know what we must do to be saved, but we can't know if we've done it! Sadly that is where most people in Christianity are today. If you can't be sure you've done what is necessary to be saved, then certainty is clearly impossible.

Clairol had an advertising tag line that read, "Only your hair-dresser knows for sure." Chantry seems to have borrowed from that when he writes, "Only the Spirit may answer the last with certainty." Only the Holy Spirit knows who has done what is necessary to be saved.

Dr. Chantry is very committed to serving God, as are all the people cited in this book. He teaches what he believes—that certainty is heretical. His book on the gospel is a best seller. Some reviewers hail it as a Christian classic. And yet, sadly, this popular view is moving multitudes away from assurance.

Anyone who embraces Chantry's position will come away saying, "Only God knows who is truly saved. We'll find out after we die."

I'm so glad I no longer have to live that way. It's wonderful to know I am eternally secure. My great aim in life is to help as many people as possible gain this same certainty.

Once you know you are His, gratitude wells up in you and you have a mission in life. You want to tell everyone that Jesus guarantees eternal life to all who simply believe in Him.

[1] Walter Chantry, *Today's Gospel: Authentic or Synthetic?* (Carlisle, PA: Banner of Truth Trust, 1970), p. 67. Note: This book has been reprinted many times, most recently in 1996.

[2] Jesus did *implicitly* call him to faith for eternal life. See note 3 below.

[3] Jesus did offer the rich young ruler assurance, though it wasn't explicitly eternal life that He promised him. Jesus said, "Sell all that you have and distribute to the poor, *and you will have treasure in heaven*" (Luke 18:22, italics added). The promise is more than eternal life. It is eternal treasure. Clearly Jesus, being omniscient, knew that this particular young man would not give up all at His promise of treasure in heaven unless he was first convinced that Jesus was indeed the Messiah who guarantees eternal life to all who simply believe in Him. Thus even assurance of eternal life by faith alone is *implicitly* offered here.

[4] Chantry, *Today's Gospel*, p. 68.

[5] Ibid., pp. 75-76, italics added.

[6] Ibid., p. 76.

[7] Ibid.

— Chapter 21 —

MANAGEABLE DISCOMFORT

D r. Richard Belcher, Bible college professor and author of
A Layman's Guide to the Lordship Controversy, spoke a few
years ago on a Dallas radio talk show. I called in and asked him a
few questions about assurance. The following is a transcript from
a tape of the show giving my questions and his answers.

CERTAINTY IMPOSSIBLE PRIOR TO DEATH

Here is how the interview began:

> BW: Is it possible for any Christian to have 100 percent cer-
> tainty that they are saved and that they can't lose it…?[1]
>
> RB: Well, the question is, can anyone have 150 percent def-
> inite, positive you know [assurance].
>
> BW: Right, that's my question.

Dr. Belcher's response began with a bit of hyperbole (150 percent) and a suggestion that what I'm asking is unreasonable. The implication is that surely everyone recognizes that certainty about one's eternal destiny is not possible.

Such thinking disturbs me because I thought like that for years and it caused ongoing agony. It disturbs me even more when the person making this statement is training young people for vocational Christian work.[2]

ASSURANCE IS ALWAYS TINGED WITH DOUBTS

RB: Well, my question is, can even the one who is walking with the Lord and knows the Lord and is submitted to the Lord and is full of God's Spirit [have such absolute certainty]?—He will have *an* assurance but that is not to say that there will never be any questions of doubt. But the Spirit of God overcomes the questions of doubt and grants assurance. See, what you're doing is putting assurance in the category of percentages and I don't like to do that.

It is commonly suggested today that assurance is always tinged with doubts—"even the one who is walking with the Lord and knows the Lord and is submitted to the Lord and is full of God's Spirit."

The appeal is sometimes made, as here, that "the Spirit of God overcomes the questions of doubt and grants assurance." However, taken in the context of what has been said before and what will follow, it is clear that something less than certainty is in view. In other words, when doubts come, even a believer in fellowship with God is bothered so that he is, to say the least, worried and distracted. Then the Spirit of God lessens the degree of concern and "assurance" is regained. Assurance in this system is a manageable level of discomfort.

Dr. Belcher makes this clear when he says, "See, what you're doing is putting assurance in the category of percentages and I don't like to do that." For him assurance is never 100 percent.

WE WILL ALWAYS HAVE DOUBT

BW: Are you 100 percent completely sure that you are going to heaven?

RB: I have *an* assurance that I am saved, but I am still in this body and I am human and in the passing of time there can be some questions in one's mind, but the Spirit of God witnesses to my spirit that I'm saved.

The reason I like to ask this question is because it reveals a lot about a person's view of the gospel and assurance.

Once again, an appeal is made to "*an* assurance" that is less than certainty. It is a poor assumption that the professors training young men and women in Bible colleges and seminaries are certain they are eternally secure. Actually, the opposite is true. Most are not, and are attempting to teach their students that doubts and fears are actually a good thing since they motivate us to do our best to persevere.

Even so, there is a reluctance to leave the issue there. Notice how the speaker says once again that the Spirit helps him out when he has doubts: "But the Spirit of God witnesses to my spirit that I'm saved." Of course, whatever this inner witness is, it is not certainty, for that is the specific question to which he is responding. Note how a simple yes or no answer is not given.

I've had conversations with many Bible college and seminary professors who have said the same thing. They aren't sure. And if you are persuaded by their teaching, then you won't be sure either.

SELF-EXAMINATION IS VITAL

BW: Is it possible that you're not saved?

RB: Well, there are various means whereby I look at my life to see if I give evidence of salvation. Not only the witness of the Holy Spirit, but there are other means whereby I look to see if I'm saved, like Paul says in 2 Corinthians 13: "Examine yourselves whether you're in the faith." And I seek to do that—as well as the witness and testimony of the Holy Spirit.

After hearing that answer, especially in light of all that he had said earlier, I was convinced he believed it was possible he himself wasn't saved. Why didn't he just admit that openly?

I believe one reason could be that this is an unpalatable aspect of the Christian theology of many today. It's hard to come right out and say you aren't sure you are regenerate and no one can be prior to death. That sounds so depressing, so uncertain, and so fatalistic. Hence, people temporize with statements about examining their works and their feelings.

If good works are indispensable for assurance, as most today believe, then certainty is indeed impossible. No matter how godly one is today, he is not, as Dr. Belcher acknowledges, perfect: "I am still in the body and I am human." We are left with assurance that includes doubts.

I consider assurance of salvation to be *the certain knowledge that I am eternally secure.* Thus there is no room in biblical assurance for doubts or degrees. If I'm not certain, then I don't have assurance.

I often joke in public preaching that the more theological education a person has, the less likely it is that he is sure he has eternal life. People laugh, but they get my point. The more theological education we receive, the greater the danger that we will become confused. Since the vast majority of professors in Christian schools don't believe in certainty, neither do the vast majority of graduates.

Doubts about eternal life come from looking at your works or your feelings. Assurance is found in looking afresh to the Lord Jesus and what He has promised to all who simply believe in Him: "He who believes in Me has everlasting life" (John 6:47).

A LAYMAN'S GUIDE TO THE LORDSHIP CONTROVERSY[3]

It would be surprising if what Dr. Belcher said on radio differed from what he said in his book. And there is no surprise of that sort. We find the same concept of assurance as manageable doubt in his book. This can be seen in his handling of two passages.

Second Corinthians 13:5

In this verse Paul says, "Examine yourselves as to whether you are in the faith. Prove yourselves. Do you not know yourselves, that Jesus Christ is in you?—unless indeed you are disqualified." Commenting on this verse and Paul's call to examine ourselves to see if we are in the faith, Belcher says:

> It should be no surprise if Paul challenges the minority of trouble-makers to be sure they are saved. *In fact, there is a possibility and there may be*

a need for any professing believer whose life is questionable to be challenged to examine the reality of his salvation, unless a preconceived system of theology disallows it.[4]

Note that *any professing believer whose life is questionable* has good reason to wonder if he or she is truly born again. And how does a person know if his life is questionable?

For the sensitive person, no matter how godly he is, his life is always questionable. If a person is concerned about the sins he sees in his life, then under this way of thinking, he would constantly doubt whether he was truly born again or not.

Indeed, would not this sort of teaching bring out doubts that didn't exist before? A person who knew he was born again by Jesus' promise that "he who believes in Me has everlasting life" would not be concerned about his eternal destiny, for Jesus guarantees it. But if you can convince that person it takes some special kind of faith to qualify for this promise, he begins to worry. And if you tell him that the way he finds out if he has the special (saving) faith, or just everyday (non-saving) faith, is by examining the quality of his life, doubts are sure to escalate. Whose life isn't questionable in light of a perfect God?

Did you notice that the only way one won't have doubts about his assurance is "unless a preconceived system of theology disallows it"? Here he is alluding to the teachings of Zane Hodges whom he just cited in his book.

What Dr. Belcher does not say is that there is another possibility. What if the teachings of the apostle Paul himself make it clear that all who simply believe in Jesus have eternal life (Romans 8:17a; 1 Corinthians 6:15-20; Galatians 2:16; Ephesians 2:8-9; Philippians 4:3)? Then Belcher would need to end his statement about doubts differently by saying "unless *Paul's doctrine disallows it, which it does.*" The idea that believers can and should be absolutely sure they have eternal life is not some man-made system of theology. It is the teaching of Jesus and His apostles.

First Corinthians 6:9-11

Belcher finds proof in this passage that once a person comes to faith he is incapable of living a sinful lifestyle.

> The fact that salvation results in a breaking with sin and a godly walk is established clearly by Paul in verse 11 of I Corinthians 6, which states, "And such were some of you: But you are washed, but you are sanctified, but you are justified in the name of the Lord Jesus, and by the Spirit of God." Paul says that some of you Corinthians were of the various sinful life-styles named in verses 9-10, but now you are washed, sanctified, and justified in the name of the Lord Jesus and by the Spirit of God. They were these things—that is, they possessed such life-styles before salvation—but not now. The "but" here is the strong adversative in the Greek. It sets off their present life-style against the former life-style. It does not allow Hodges' definition of saving faith which results in no change of life-style. Neither does it allow his attempt to define inheriting the kingdom as a separate category from entering it. Again, we will leave it to the readers to decide whose interpretation is unfair to the text, hopelessly confused, and extremely careless.[5]

If salvation (by which Dr. Belcher means *regeneration*) necessarily results in 1) breaking with sin, and 2) a godly walk, then logically anyone who is imperfect has every reason to doubt he is born again.

It's easy to see how in this way of thinking no living person can be certain he has eternal life. Even if one's current walk is without question godly and free from any particular besetting sin, no one could be sure that his walk would continue as it was at that moment. People do fall away. The Bible warns of this. No one can be sure that he himself is or will be free from a sinful lifestyle. Thus, for Belcher, certainty is impossible.

And it should be noted that few if any professing Christians would be so bold to say that they are certain they have broken from sin and their walk is godly. If we continue to sin repeatedly (1 John 1:8, 10), under this way of thinking, one would be inclined to conclude that either breaking from sin is God grading on the curve, or else no one is born again.

The way Dr. Belcher explains verse 11 is not the only way the text can be understood. Indeed, it is not even the way most commentators understand it.

Clearly when Paul speaks of the fact that the Corinthian believers had been *justified*, he was not talking about their current or former *lifestyles*. The fact they had been justified did not, in and of itself, indicate they were living righteously, unless, of course, one believes that justification is *imparted righteousness*. Indeed, one cannot read the first five chapters of the book and conclude that Paul considered his readers to be living righteously.

Additionally, the term *washed* does not refer to a change in lifestyle. It refers to spiritual cleansing, which is forgiveness (as in Titus 3:5, "washing of regeneration").

Finally, Paul's reference to being *sanctified* (past tense) looks not at *present* progressive sanctification, but at *past* positional sanctification. The believers in Corinth had been set apart once and for all into God's family.

Earlier in the book Belcher suggested that Paul made a godly lifestyle indispensable for assurance. He wrote:

> Assurance of salvation is a great blessing and encouragement to the believer, and Scripture gives glorious promise of God's power to save and keep. Yet the believer should not take his salvation for granted nor presume upon the grace of God. Scripture challenges us to examine ourselves to see that we are in the faith. The evidence we are His is the presence of a holy and godly life and godly works. *The absence of such should cause deep and serious examination of life* to see if we really have experienced saving faith. Such examination should result in a renewed commitment to godliness or in a true experience of salvation and saving faith.[6]

This is a rather remarkable statement. Note the result of self-examination should be that the professor, one who doesn't know if he is born again or not, gains either "a renewed commitment to godliness," or else "a true experience of salvation and saving faith."

One could see how self-examination could lead to a renewed commitment to godliness. However, how can examining one's works lead to "a true experience of salvation and saving faith"? If one already believes correct doctrine, then the issue cannot be what he believes, but what he does. Self-examination of one's works might cause a person to work harder for God. But unless working harder for God is a condition for eternal life, one could not experience salvation and saving faith as a result of examining his works.[7]

And how does a professing believer know whether he needs "a renewed commitment to godliness" or "a true experience of salvation and saving faith"? If either option is viable each time one examines himself, it would seem that a person would be confused about his standing with God until the day he died and was released from this agonizing concern.

A Manageable Level of Discomfort

Both in his radio conversation with me and in his book, Dr. Belcher asserts that one cannot be certain he is born again prior to death. All who profess faith in Christ are just that, professors. Whether they are true or false professors will not be certain until death occurs. At that time some will find themselves in the flames of Sheol and will thereby presumably know that they were false professors all along. Others will regain consciousness in heaven and will rejoice that at last they can be certain they have eternal life.

I am grieved that people are willing to live with discomfort their entire lives about whether they are God's children or not. It saddens me that those who are teaching the next generation of pastors and missionaries think that God wants Christians to live their whole lives with doubts about their eternal destiny.

My own experience is that such thinking does not promote true godliness. It didn't cause me to view God as my loving heavenly Father. Rather, when I thought this way, I viewed God as a demanding tyrant who wished me to twist in the winds of doubt and despair until the day I died.

When I came to believe what Dr. Belcher calls "unfair to the text, hopelessly confused, and extremely careless,"[8] I found my lifestyle dramatically changed for the better, even though my external piety didn't improve much. I was a very moral unbeliever.

I didn't even hold hands with girls, much less kiss them or get involved in immorality. I'd never been drunk or even had a drink. My smoking career was one puff as a child. I didn't swear at all. I thought if I did any of these things, or indeed sin in any way, I'd lose my salvation and could never regain it.

What changed dramatically in my lifestyle when I came to faith was my attitude about myself and others. I lost my self-righteous attitude. I stopped treating others as though they were spiritually inferior to me. I started to recognize that I had lots of anger toward my father, and then I started confessing it.

It wasn't long before for the first time in my life, I said, "I love you, Dad."

My life did not go down the drain when I became sure of eternal life by faith alone apart from works, and apart from any self-examination. It zoomed when I gave up such thinking.

Of course, everyone has their experience. Experience does not prove that one's doctrine is correct. However, the idea that certainty is harmful to one's spiritual health is not true in my experience, nor in the experience of thousands upon thousands of people I have met. The opposite is true. Experience shows that certainty produces gratitude which in turn produces godliness.

---

[1] I left out the end of my question since I was tongue-tied when I started. Here is the entirety of my initial question: "Is it possible for any Christian to have 100 percent certainty that they are saved and that they can't lose it if the quality of my lifestyle has something to do with my assurance? In other words, can I be absolutely sure that I'm saved?" I shouldn't have shifted from the third person to the first person in the midst of the question.

[2] Dr. Belcher is Director of the Pastoral Ministries Program at Columbia International University (formerly Columbia Bible College) in South Carolina.

[3] Richard P. Belcher, *A Layman's Guide to the Lordship Controversy* (Southbridge, MA: Crowne Publications, 1990).

[4] Ibid., p. 88, italics added.

[5] Ibid., pp. 91-92.

[6] Ibid., p. 56, italics added.

[7] Of course, if by examining one's works a person realized he would never be good enough, this might move him to cry out to God. Then God might open his heart to the truth of justification by faith apart from works. However, this is clearly not what Dr. Belcher means.

[8] Belcher, *Layman's Guide*, p. 92.

— Chapter 22 —

UNCERTAINTY IS BETTER THAN ANY OTHER OPTION

Founder and chairman of Ligonier Ministries, Dr. R.C. Sproul is a well-known author, educator, conference speaker, and radio preacher. The following information about him appears at the Ligonier website:

> Dr. R.C. Sproul is the founder and chairman of Ligonier Ministries and can be heard teaching daily on the "Renewing Your Mind" radio broadcast on more than 300 radio outlets in the United States and throughout 120 countries. He holds degrees from Westminster College, Pittsburgh Theological Seminary, the Free University of Amsterdam, and Whitefield Theological Seminary. He has written more than 50 books and has authored scores of magazine articles for evangelical publications. In addition, he has taught at numerous colleges and seminaries.[1]

Needless to say, Dr. Sproul is well educated, bright, and a strong leader. Thus what he has to say about assurance is especially significant. In a November 1989 article in Ligonier's monthly magazine, *TableTalk*, he described his personal struggles with assurance in a very poignant way. I have broken what he had to say into four sections.

STRUGGLING WITH ASSURANCE

False Professors Rob Genuine Believers of Assurance

Dr. Sproul began his article on assurance this way:

> There are people in this world who are not saved, but who are convinced that they are. The presence of such people causes genuine Christians to doubt their salvation. After all, we wonder, suppose I am in that category? Suppose I am mistaken about my salvation and am really going to hell? How can I know that I am a real Christian?

If you are unfamiliar with Reformed theology, what he is saying here doesn't make sense. Sproul is a five-point Calvinist. He believes that you can't be sure if you truly believe in Jesus until you die. This is because he sees faith in Christ as much more than simply being convinced He gives eternal life to the believer. Saving faith includes commitment and repentance and results in obedience and lifelong perseverance. Since those things are subjective, and since future perseverance is uncertain, certainty is impossible.

Many of us believe that false professors exist and yet are not at all bothered in terms of our own assurance. We know we believe in Jesus and that all who do so are eternally secure.

If everyone who *professed* to be a Christian really was, then Reformed theologians like Sproul wouldn't have to struggle with assurance. Of course, if there were no false professors, then Reformed theology would need modification, since the concept of false professors is a central tenet of that theological position.

Thus whenever a person who believes that certainty is not an option reflects on the existence of false professors, he is drowned in a tidal wave of fear and doubt. That is exactly the point which Sproul goes on to make.

Self-awareness Can Cause Doubts

> A while back I had one of those moments of acute self-awareness that we have from time to time, and suddenly the question hit me: "R.C., what if you are not one of the redeemed? What if your destiny is not heaven after all, but hell?" Let me tell you that I was flooded in my body with a chill that went from my head to the bottom of my spine. I was terrified.

This is a very candid statement by a highly visible Christian leader. From time to time self-awareness strikes all of us, R.C. says, and that results in chilling, all-consuming, terror that we may be bound for an eternity of torment in hell.

The reason why introspection results in terror for those who believe as Dr. Sproul does is because certainty is impossible prior to death. No one can know if he is one of those for whom Christ died. Sproul believes that Christ died only for the elect. And he believes you can't be sure you are elect until you die. Terror is thus a reasonable emotion.

Seemingly there would be no way to escape this terror prior to death. It would appear that developing a fatalistic attitude and trying to divert your attention to other things would be the only way to deal with these fears. Let's see how Sproul dealt with his own fears on that occasion.

Doubts Not Soothed by Works

> I tried to grab hold of myself. I thought, "Well, it's a good sign that I'm worried about this. Only true Christians really care about salvation." But then I began to take stock of my life, and I looked at my performance. My sins came pouring into my mind, and the more I looked at myself, the worse I felt. I thought, "Maybe it's really true. Maybe I'm not saved after all."

Many authors today give a number of tests to help you determine if you are born again. Sproul here rejects the idea that self-examination of commitment or obedience or anything else was going to eliminate his fear of hell. His comments here are refreshingly honest. If these tests are subjective in nature, then certainty is impossible. I'm glad to see a Reformed theologian candidly admit such tests can't produce certainty.

Two tests people typically cite are the one's Dr. Sproul mentions here: concern about spiritual things (especially salvation), and the works that we do under the enabling ministry of the Holy Spirit. Sproul cuts through all that and acknowledges that our sins trump our commitment and our works. If we are sinners, then unless Jesus died for us, we are hopeless. No amount of commitment or works can save us or prove we are saved.

Being Uncomfortable Is the Best Option

> I went to my room and began to read the Bible. On my knees I said, "Well, here I am. I can't point

to my obedience. There's nothing I can offer. I can only rely on Your atonement for my sins. I can only throw myself on Your mercy." Even then I knew that some people only flee to the Cross to escape hell, not out of a real turning to God. I could not be sure about my own heart and motivation. Then I remembered John 6:68. Jesus had been giving out hard teaching, and many of His former followers had left Him. When He asked Peter if he was also going to leave, Peter said, "Where else can I go? Only You have the words of eternal life." In other words, Peter was also uncomfortable, but he realized that being uncomfortable with Jesus was better than any other option!

Prayer is a valid response to such terror. Why not pray and ask God to show you from His Word if it is possible to be certain, and if so, how? Unfortunately, R.C. is convinced certainty is impossible, so he doesn't pray for that. In his prayer he reminds God of his sinful condition and throws himself on God's mercy.

Sproul indicates that it is wrong to "flee to the Cross to escape hell." But isn't that a valid reason to believe in Jesus? Isn't that what Jesus Himself said in His most famous saying (John 3:16)? He said that whoever believes in Him would not perish. He repeatedly promised no condemnation for those who simply believe in Him (John 3:18; 5:24; 6:35-40; 11:26).

Sproul assumes that Peter was expressing doubts about his assurance. Yet is that a reasonable understanding of what Peter said? "Lord, to whom shall we go? You have the words of eternal life." Unless *words of eternal life* means something like "the message of what one must do to gain eternal life," Sproul's conclusion misses Peter's point entirely. Eternal life in Scripture and in John's

Gospel is more than merely spiritual life of unending duration. It is also God's life (cf. John 14:6, "I am the life"). As such, it is a life full of potential: "I have come that they might have life, and that they might have it more abundantly" (John 10:10b).

Peter already had eternal life and he was sure of that (compare John 1:41-42; 2:11; 3:16-18; 5:24; 6:35-40, 47). He wanted to know what he was to do with that life. How should eternal life be lived this side of glory? The Lord Jesus, better than any teacher of all time, could and did answer that question. Why would Peter go anywhere else? The fact that many of Jesus' disciples were leaving didn't tempt Peter to leave.

Peter was not "uncomfortable with Jesus." And that is not the best option.

Of course, five-point Calvinism doesn't allow for a better option than uncertainty. Sproul is right if the Westminster Confession is correct about assurance.

But what if the Westminster Confession is wrong on this point? What if God wants us to be absolutely sure we are eternally secure? In that case we would no longer be subject to the terror he describes. Would there not be a tremendous sense of relief and gratitude?

An Update on Sproul's Views

Admittedly that was fifteen years ago. To be fair to Dr. Sproul, we ought to consider what he's said about assurance since then.

Grace Unknown

Grace Unknown: The Heart of Reformed Theology[2] is a book copyrighted in 1997 and in its fourth printing in 2000. It is, as its subtitle suggests, an explanation of Reformed theology.

There are about 18 pages on assurance in this book (pp. 199-216). Here we find some of the same things mentioned in the 1989 *TableTalk* article.

> The [Westminster] confession acknowledges that there is such a thing as false assurance...
>
> The apostle [Peter, in 2 Peter 1:10-12] calls us to pursue assurance with diligence. It is the assurance of our election, which translates to assurance of our salvation. All of the elect are saved,[3] so if we can be sure that we are the elect, we can also be sure that we are saved. To what end does the apostle exhort us to make our election sure? "If you do these things," he says, "you will never stumble"...
>
> One thing, however, is certain. There is a clear link between our assurance and our sanctification.[4]

Yet notice these indications that certainty is not only possible, but expected:

> The person who lacks assurance of salvation is vulnerable to a myriad of threats to his personal growth. [Amen!] The confident Christian, *certain of his salvation*, is free from the paralyzing fear that can inhibit personal growth. Without assurance we are assailed by doubt and uncertainty with respect to God's promises, which serve as an anchor for our souls. [Amen!]
>
> It is of utmost importance that new Christians *become certain of their personal salvation*. Such assurance is a mighty boon to the growth of faith to maturity.[5]

Twice Sproul speaks of the possibility and desirability of being "certain of salvation." Unfortunately, what follows doesn't show how anyone can be certain. Sproul says that four things produce certainty: "the promises of God, the internal testimony of the Holy Spirit, the earnest of the Spirit, and the sealing of the Spirit."[6] Yet the inner witness of the Spirit is subjective. And the earnest and sealing of the Spirit are indiscernible experientially. One might as well speak of regeneration as proof of regeneration! How, apart from believing the objective promises to the believer, does one know he has been sealed by the Holy Spirit?

Indeed, the next section of the book is entitled, "Assurance and Sanctification." There Sproul says,

> Assurance is not frozen in concrete, incapable of augmentation or diminution. Our faith and assurance tend to be fragile. Assurance can be easily disrupted and rudely shaken. It can be intermittent. It is particularly vulnerable to sin.[7]

He then continues,

> What Christian has not undergone what Martin Luther called the *Anfectung*, the "unbridled assault" of Satan? We are faced daily with manifold temptations, some of them grievous in nature and intensity, and we all too often succumb to them. Sin is the great enemy of assurance. When we commit it, we ask ourselves, "How can a true Christian do such things?" Then we must flee to Christ in confession and repentance, seeking his pardon and finding our solace in the Consolation of Israel. He alone can restore us to the joy of our salvation and the assurance of it.[8]

If when we sin we go through doubts as to whether we are "true Christians," then how could one ever be certain? After all, we all sin over and over again (1 John 1:8, 10).

In the next paragraph Sproul says, "We can feel totally abandoned by God, and in our spirit we may approach the rim of the abyss of hell."[9] That sounds about as far from certainty as one can possibly be. If that is an ongoing experience for all Christians, then certainty would seem to be something that must await our departure from this body when we cease sinning.

The next section in *Grace Unknown* is entitled "Perseverance in Salvation." Sproul says,

> We have seen the close link between the assurance of salvation and perseverance in the Christian life...
>
> We have all known people who have made professions of faith and exhibited zeal for Christ, only to repudiate their confessions and turn away from Christ. What should we make of this? We consider two possibilities.
>
> The first possibility is that their profession was not genuine in the first place, They confessed Christ with their mouths and then later committed a real apostasy from that confession...They gave some outward signs of conversion, but their conversion was not genuine...
>
> The second possible explanation...is that they are true believers who have fallen into serious and radical apostasy, but who will repent of their sin and be restored before they die. If they persist in apostasy until death, then theirs is a full and final fall from grace, which is evidence that they were not genuine believers in the first place.[10]

Since no one can be sure he will persevere in the future, not even the apostle Paul (1 Corinthians 9:27), under this way of thinking, could be certain he was born again prior to death. Only after persevering to death could one discern whether he was a true believer or not.

The Soul's Quest for God

This is a book that was copyrighted in 1992 and reissued in 2003 by P & R Publishing Company.[11] Again Dr. Sproul goes back to some of the themes found in his 1989 *TableTalk* article.

Note this amazing statement: "It is possible both to be saved and to know that we are saved, and to *be unsaved and be sure that we are saved.*"[12] This leads him to the logical question, "[Then] how can we know in which category we truly are?"

He next discusses various reasons why people might be "unsaved and yet sure that they are saved."

Dr. Sproul addresses people with "false views of salvation,"[13] where he discusses four wrong understandings of what we must do to have eternal life.

He also considers those with "faulty self-analysis." Sproul says we must take care that we truly love Christ.[14] He also says that we must examine our works:

> No fruit means no faith. Some fruit means some faith. The Bible tells us we will know them by their fruit…The indispensable evidence of true faith is the presence of works. The works add nothing to the merit of Christ, by whose merit we are justified. But faith inevitably and necessarily produces works or it is not saving faith.[15]

Of course, there's the rub. If one ceases to do good works, or if one doubts that his works are good enough, or if he sees in his works a mixture of good and bad, then he can't be sure he has eternal life, for "the *indispensable* evidence of true faith is the presence of works."[16] When one's works are less than perfect, he has good reason to doubt that he has what Sproul calls "true faith."

Later he says,

> It is not the person who professes faith who is saved; it is the one who does the will of the Father.
>
> Works that are evidence of true faith are not merely activities of the church or ministry; they are works of obedience. We can be engaged in church or religious activities for all sorts of evil motives. Such works, even when God makes good use of them, do not please him. What pleases him is a genuine spirit of obedience, which is the fruit of genuine faith.[17]

If our motives are often wrong, then how do we know our works are truly ones that show we are born again? After all, if "God makes use of" the works of false professors in the church, would not we be left in uncertainty? Wouldn't we be back to the fact that "being uncomfortable with Jesus [is] better than any other option" as he said in *TableTalk?* It would seem so.

CERTAINTY WITH JESUS

To say that the very best option available is "being uncomfortable with Jesus" is theology gone awry. There is a better option. Simply believe Jesus when He promises, "He who believes in Me has everlasting life" (John 6:47). It's that simple. Don't get hung up on theological systems. Don't look to your works for proof you are born again. Don't look for some feeling that indicates you are regenerate.

The Scriptures are clear. We can and should take them at face value. This may mean we must abandon the theology we've grown up under—at least in part. If so, that is what we should do. For being *certain* with Jesus is better than any other option.

---

[1] See http://www.ligonier.org/history.php.

[2] R.C. Sproul, *Grace Unknown: The Heart of Reformed Theology* (Grand Rapids: Baker Books, 1997).

[3] He means, of course, that all of the elect will eventually be regenerated. Obviously there are elect people who have not yet come to faith and are not yet saved. Some elect people haven't even been born yet.

[4] Sproul, *Grace Unknown*, pp. 199-200.

[5] Ibid., pp. 200-201, italics added.

[6] Ibid., p. 202.

[7] Ibid., p. 204.

[8] Ibid., p. 205.

[9] Ibid.

[10] Ibid., pp. 207-209.

[11] R.C. Sproul, *The Soul's Quest for God: Satisfying the Hunger for Spiritual Communion with God* (Phillipsburg, NJ: P&R Publishing, 1992).

[12] Ibid., p. 213, italics added.

[13] Ibid., pp. 215-16.

[14] Ibid., p. 216.

[15] Ibid., pp. 217-18.

[16] Ibid., p. 218, italics added.

[17] Ibid., p. 225.

— Chapter 23 —

A MYRIAD OF FACTORS
TO CONSIDER

John MacArthur pastors the 7,000-member Grace Community Church in Southern California. He has authored scores of books and is the host of the popular *Grace to You* radio program, heard on thousands of stations around the world. He is also the President of The Master's College and The Master's Seminary.

In 1989 he was a keynote speaker at the annual meeting of the Evangelical Theological Society in San Diego, California. I was in the audience that day.

His message was on saving faith and what he had to say touched on assurance. After he finished his message, he fielded questions from the audience.

I was able to ask him a few questions on the issue of assurance and specifically if a person could be 100 percent sure that he was saved. He responded by saying that "there is no way to quantify that [assurance] because everybody is different, and there are a myriad of factors which deal with that..."

His reply struck me as an admission that one can't be certain. His subsequent remarks clarified what he was really saying:

> I personally believe that since the fruit of the Spirit is love, joy, peace, and so forth, inherent in that is certain confidences about my position before God. And if I am exercising my flesh and living in disobedience, I may not enjoy the fullness of that. So to say that you could reach a point that you are one hundred percent sure of your salvation *permanently* would be very difficult to deal with scripturally.

In other words, he seemed to imply that a person could be 100 percent sure *for a time* (although he stopped short of saying that), but not permanently. In MacArthur's view assurance is not based solely on the promises God makes to those who believe in Jesus. Rather, he sees "a myriad of factors" that influence assurance. The result is that "there is no way to quantify that because everybody is different."

But that was 1989. In order to delve into Dr. MacArthur's understanding of assurance further, I have consulted some of his writings since then. What follows suggests, as do the comments cited above, that on the one hand, he wishes to say that certainty is possible for periods of time when presumably one is living a godly life. On the other hand, he wants to avoid giving the impression that one can ever reach a point of confidence that he is eternally secure regardless of his future behavior. Fear of hell seems to be an essential part of the Christian's motivation to live for God.

FEATURES OF TRUE ASSURANCE

In the Winter 2003 issue of *The Master's Seminary Mantle*, MacArthur wrote about "Features of True Christian Assurance." In the article he discussed three types of assurance: cognitive, subjective, and behavioral.

Cognitive assurance according to MacArthur is the assurance that comes when we believe the gospel.

> The moment you trust Christ in salvation, you know the Bible promises that you are saved by grace through faith and therefore you know that you are saved.[1]

He went on to say:

> But the cognitive assurance we have in the act of faith, based on the promises of Scripture, is not perfect or full (Mk 9:24; Lk 17:5; Heb 10:22). In addition to the cognitive element, there is a subjective element of assurance that comes by the witness of the Holy Spirit in us. And there's a third element: the behavioral assurance—how we live our lives. All three contribute to full assurance.[2]

There you have it. The promises of the Bible are not sufficient to have "full assurance"—whatever that means.[3] What "full assurance" is, isn't clear. But what *is* clear is that anything less is obviously not certainty.

Subjective assurance according to MacArthur comes through five means: experiencing God's leading and direction in one's life, intimacy with God, having a clear conscience, conviction of sin, and experiencing God's chastening for sin.[4] Of course, all but one of those things are subjective. One cannot be sure that he is being led and directed by God, that he is intimate with God, that he has a clear conscience, or that the difficulties he is experiencing in life are proofs of God's chastening of one of His children as opposed to His judgment of an unbeliever.

Behavioral assurance is obedience that, for Dr. MacArthur, is objective:

> This [1 John 2:3-5] is objective visible proof that you're a Christian—obedience. That is the behavioral test by which you can know you are a believer (cf. 1 John 5:13). There is no assurance of salvation apart from sanctification![5]

Personally I find it hard to see how obedience is objective. The only way it could be objective is if it were quantifiable. For example, if the Bible said, "He who reads aloud every word of John 3:16 has everlasting life," then if you could read every word aloud, you'd be sure. However, there is no such objective obedience standard in the Bible.

Summing it all up, it would seem that since all three of these are needed for "full assurance" and since two of these are subjective in nature, then it would be impossible to be certain. Yet MacArthur also has an entire book on assurance called *Saved Without a Doubt: How to Be Sure of Your Salvation*. Let's see what he says there.

SAVED WITHOUT A DOUBT[6]

Unfortunately the book doesn't deliver what the title and subtitle promise. In the section titled "How You Can Tell Whether You Are Truly a Christian," the author cites "Eleven Tests from an Apostolic Expert." The following eleven tests derived from First

John are presented as the means by which one can be sure he is regenerate:

1. Have you enjoyed fellowship with Christ and the Father?[7]
2. Are you sensitive to sin?[8]
3. Do you obey God's Word?[9]
4. Do you reject this evil world?[10]
5. Do you eagerly await Christ's return?[11]
6. Do you see a decreasing pattern of sin in your life?[12]
7. Do you love other Christians?[13]
8. Do you experience answered prayer?[14]
9. Do you experience the ministry of the Holy Spirit?[15]
10. Can you discern between spiritual truth and error?[16]
11. Have you suffered rejection because of your faith?[17]

As you can see, it is impossible to answer many of these questions with certainty—unless you are first sure you are a child of God.[18]

In the first place, these questions are very broad and subjective. For example, what about someone who finds that he loves some Christians, but not others? What of the person who receives answers to some prayers, but has many more unanswered? What if you haven't experienced much rejection for your faith? Or what if you've experienced rejection, but you aren't sure if it is because of your faith or a result of bad people skills? How do you decide if you are sinning less and less? Since no one is perfectly obedient (1 John 1:8, 10), how do you know if you are obedient *enough?* If you are sometimes distracted by worldly concerns (job, taxes, family, etc.), does that mean you are not truly eager for Christ's return?

In the second place, is it not possible for people to convince themselves that they pass these eleven tests, and yet for these same people not to believe in justification by faith apart from works? Isn't that what the Lord is addressing in Matthew 7:21-23? Tests like the ones MacArthur suggests—if used for the purpose of discerning whether you are born again—actually motivate unbelieving legalists to rationalize away their sins, take an optimistic view of their works, and move towards a false sense that maybe they are going to make it. Assurance can never be grounded in the works we do in Jesus' name (Matthew 7:22).

ONLY ONE FACTOR

There really is only one test for assurance. Was Jesus telling the truth when He promised, "He who believes in Me has everlasting life" (John 6:47)? If I believe He was, then I know I have everlasting life. Indeed, that was Jesus' question to Martha in John 11:26. Martha in her answer did not cite her works, her love for other believers, her conviction of sin, or any of the other supposed myriad of factors. Instead, she affirmed her faith in Jesus as the resurrection and the life. She was sure because the evidence of His miraculous signs and His sinless life convinced her. Assurance is all about Jesus and His works and not at all about us and our works.

There is but one factor, one test, and one Way. His name is Jesus.

---

[1] John MacArthur, "Features of True Christian Assurance," *The Master's Seminary Mantle* (Winter 2003): p. 1.

[2] Ibid.

[3] "Full Assurance" is an expression most Reformed writers use. However, it is rarely if ever explained. What is "full assurance"? It appears to be the maximum amount of probability possible. But even "full assurance" is less than certainty.

[4] MacArthur, "Features of True Christian Assurance," p. 4.

[5] Ibid.

[6] John MacArthur, *Saved Without a Doubt: How to Be Sure of Your Salvation* (Wheaton, IL: Victor Books, 1992).

[7] Ibid., pp. 69-70.

[8] Ibid., pp. 70-72.

[9] Ibid., pp. 72-73.

[10] Ibid., pp. 73-75.

[11] Ibid., pp. 75-76.

[12] Ibid., pp. 76-79.

[13] Ibid., pp. 79-83.

[14] Ibid., pp. 83-84.

[15] Ibid., pp. 85-86.

[16] Ibid., pp. 86-89.

[17] Ibid, pp. 89-91.

[18] If I know with certainty that I am a child of God because I believe in Jesus for eternal life, then I could potentially be certain, for example, that I have experienced rejection because of my faith. But I must know I have faith before I can be sure that the persecution is really for Christ and not for my own false doctrine. If I'm sure I'm born again, I can also know I'm in fellowship with God if I am walking in the light of God's Word and confessing my sins as I become aware of them (1 John 1:5-10). But if the promises of God don't give me certainty, then how could I hope to know I was in fellowship with God?

Conclusion

So are you sure? Do you know with certainty that you are eternally secure?

Do you grasp this truth well enough to share it with others? If so, I strongly urge you to do so this very day.

Email someone about the great joy you have in knowing you are eternally secure simply by faith in Jesus.

Write a letter to a friend or family member. Call someone. Tell someone at work or school or church.

I urge you to apply what you've learned in this book. Why not go to your pastor and ask if you could teach a Sunday School class on this subject? Whether you were teaching elementary school children, middle schoolers, high schoolers, college students, or adults, you'd learn the material that much better by teaching it. Plus you'd be helping others at the same time.

If you get the passion, then this will revolutionize your witnessing. Now you no longer need to struggle about how to get the conversation going. You don't need to feel like you're presenting some strange truth that people aren't really interested in hearing.

I feel the reason why evangelism is often cold and impersonal is because we take too long to get down to the heart of the matter: Jesus guarantees everlasting life to all who simply believe in Him, regardless of what happens in the future.

Lots of people aren't motivated to evangelize because they believe it is impossible to be sure where you are going until you die. Thus they know that their message isn't that appealing to others, or even to themselves.

But if you are sure, you now have the excitement that the apostles and other early Christians had. It was that certainty that led them to "turn the world upside down" as some charged them with doing (Acts 17:6).

The cross and the resurrection come into perfect focus when we realize they are not just designed to pay for our sins and make us savable. The cross and empty tomb should lead us to faith that the crucified and risen Savior guarantees everlasting life to all who simply believe in Him, with no strings attached.[1] And once we do believe in Jesus for eternal life, God is glorified. *Believers* now and forever will continue to be evidence of "the exceeding riches of His grace in His kindness toward us in Christ Jesus" (Ephesians 2:7).

To believe in the cross and resurrection of Jesus and yet not be sure that you have everlasting life is a tragic distortion of biblical truth. Sadly, the message of the cross and the empty tomb has, in many churches, been divorced from the guarantee of everlasting life to all who merely believe in Jesus.

So when you evangelize, make sure you call people to certainty. That is the promise of the good news. Tell them that the One who died and rose again guarantees everlasting life to all who simply believe in Him.

Secure and sure. That is what everyone is who believes in Jesus for everlasting life. Of course once we come to faith, we remain *secure* forever. But to remain *sure*, we must continue to believe the good news. Do that and you will have the foundation you need to persevere in a life that is pleasing to God.

We should long to hear those blessed words, "Well done, good and faithful servant." Ongoing certainty can keep us on track, aiming for His approval (1 Corinthians 9:27).

Be sure. Stay sure. And keep on sharing that good news with others.

---

[1] In addition, the cross and resurrection are designed to lead those who have believed in Jesus and have eternal life to follow Jesus' example and lay down our lives for others (e.g., 1 John 3:16-18). While the example view of the atonement (that we are born again by following Jesus' example) is wrong, the example view of sanctification (that we please God in our Christian experience by following Jesus' example) is correct.

Epilogue

Think back to the story of the five-year-old Phoenix twins which we considered in the Prologue. They were imprisoned by their parents. Their home was a makeshift cage—lonely, dark, and uncertain. This factual yet unbelievable story makes us long for an existence where things like this simply do not occur.

Sadly, life for most Christians parallels this story in a way. Jesus said, "He who believes in Me has everlasting life" (John 6:47). Yet how many people who profess to believe in Jesus nonetheless turn right around and say they aren't sure if they have everlasting life, and even say that such certainty is presumptuous?

Many committed followers of Christ[1] accept the misguided notion that no one can be sure until death that they truly possess eternal life. They are trapped in a cage that seems so strong that they give up trying to escape. They are consigned to a life of fear of hell.

May this not be true of you! God wants you to be absolutely sure that you are eternally secure simply on the basis of believing in the Lord Jesus.

I hope after having read this book, you know how to walk in the security that is reserved only for God's children. If you believe in Jesus, you are secure indeed. Jesus said, "I am the resurrection and the life. He who believes in Me, though he may die, he shall live. And whoever lives and believes in Me shall never die" (John 11:25-26a). He then asked Martha, "Do you believe this?" (John 11:26b). She did and she told Him so. Her words have been recorded for all eternity so that others may have that certainty as well.

Do *you* believe this? I *certainly* hope so!

---

[1] By "committed followers of Christ" I do *not* necessarily mean born-again people. I mean people within Christendom who are committed followers of Christ, whether they have ever believed the saving message or not.

Study Guide

The following questions are designed to be used in small groups: Sunday School classes, Bible studies, discipleship groups, family devotions, etc.

The questions are meant to be challenging, and in many cases more than one answer is correct depending on how you explain and defend your answer.

The answers are not necessarily found directly in the chapters themselves. Hopefully the material in the chapters will help you think about the issues so that you can answer questions which are merely implications of things discussed.

CHAPTER 1: CERTAINTY

1. Defend the idea that biblical assurance is certainty.
2. What are the practical ramifications of believing that a person cannot be certain he has eternal life until he dies?
3. Are you sure? If yes, why?
4. Do you believe it is possible to have eternal life and yet never to have been certain of that fact? Why or why not?
5. Define eternal security.

6. Why wouldn't a person who was sure he was eternally secure just go out and live like the devil?

7. What are the greatest hindrances to certainty in your opinion? Defend your answers.

8. Since far and away the vast majority of people in Christianity (Protestant, Catholic, Eastern Orthodox, etc.) do not believe it is possible to be certain, doesn't this suggest that certainty isn't possible? After all, how could God allow such a high percentage of people *within Christianity* to miss such a basic truth?

Chapter 2: God's Word

1. Prove from the Bible that the source of assurance is the Bible alone.

2. Why can't our works produce certainty?

3. Why can't our feelings produce certainty?

4. What's wrong with the idea that it takes all three, faith in the promises, seeing the works God is doing through us, and feeling the inner witness of the Spirit, in order to have assurance?

5. Since none of us is an infallible interpreter of the Bible, doesn't this make assurance via the Bible impossible? Why or why not?

6. Why do you think the Gospel of John might be the best place to start to find verses on assurance?

7. Name three passages in John which say that all who believe in Jesus have eternal life.

8. Since it is possible for a believer to stop believing and lose assurance, how can the passages you just mentioned provide certainty?

Chapter 3: Biblical Promises

1. Using a concordance, look up all the uses of the word *assurance* in the New Testament. Do you think that any of them deal with assurance *of regeneration* (*i.e., eternal salvation*)? Why or why not?

2. Do you find it strange that God hasn't given us special words for the Trinity, the Rapture, the hypostatic union, or certainty that we have eternal life? Why or why not?

3. Prior to reading this book, if you had tried to help a person gain assurance, what passage would have been your first choice to show them? Why?

4. Do you agree or disagree with the suggestion that gospel promises found in John's Gospel are actually the best place to start to help a person gain certainty? Why or why not?

5. Pick one of the passages cited in this chapter from John's Gospel and show how you might use it to help a person gain certainty.

6. Pick one of the "side comment passages" cited in this chapter and show how you might use it to help a person gain certainty.

7. Do you think it likely that God would want at least some first century believers to be absolutely sure they had eternal life, but no twenty-first century believers? Why or why not?

8. If it is impossible for us to know whether or not we are believers prior to death, then of what practical value are the promises in the Bible to the one who believes in Jesus?

CHAPTER 4: PRESENT FAITH

1. Why do you think so many people, when discussing their assurance, point back to what happened years ago?

2. Why can't past faith give you certainty today?

3. How is faith different than walking an aisle, praying a prayer, or making a commitment?

4. Do you think it is important to know the exact day on which you first believed? Why or why not?

5. If you can't figure out when you were born again, does that bother you? Why or why not?

6. How could a person who was certain he had eternal life ever lose that certainty?

7. To put it another way, if a person isn't sure today, doesn't that prove he has never believed in Jesus for eternal life? Why or why not?

8. Can sin cause us to lose assurance? Why or why not?

CHAPTER 5: WALKING IN ASSURANCE

1. What is discipleship?

2. Briefly argue *against* the idea that assurance is essential in order for a person to be a successful disciple.

3. Now switch positions and briefly attempt to prove that assurance is indeed essential in order to be a successful disciple.

4. Do you agree or disagree with the statement that we can only be grateful for something we are sure we have? Why or why not?

5. Name some things for which a person who lacks certainty of eternal life might nonetheless be thankful to God.

6. Is it true that legalism doesn't produce true righteousness? Why or why not?

7. Agree or disagree? If a person is not sure that simply by faith in Jesus he is eternally secure, then he is a legalist. Why or why not?

8. Do you think it's appropriate to compare the fact that loving human parents accept their children no matter what, with the knowledge that God who is love accepts all His children no matter what? Why or why not?

CHAPTER 6: THE GREATEST SOURCE OF JOY

1. Do you find more joy in what you do for Christ, or in knowing that your name is written in heaven? Why?

2. Why did Jesus tell the seventy disciples that they should rejoice in their names being written in heaven rather than in the fact that the demons were subject to them?

3. When do you think a person's name is put in the Lamb's Book of Life? Was this done in eternity past? Is it done when a person is conceived, when they are born, or when they are born again? Defend your answer.

4. How did Paul know that the names of Euodia, Syntyche, and Clement were in the Book of Life (Philippians 4:3)?

5. How does anyone today know that their name is written in the Book of Life?

6. Is it necessary to have a joyful heart in order to be effective in ministry? Why?

7. Do you think that fear of hell aids or hinders a person in serving God? Defend your answer.

8. Do you agree that there is no greater joy in life than knowing you are eternally secure? Why or why not?

Chapter 7: The Power of Gratitude

1. Define gratitude.

2. Name something you are extremely grateful for that someone did for you.

3. Did your gratitude toward that person motivate you to want to do something for them, even though nothing was required in return?

4. Why should Christians be more grateful than Buddhists, Hindus, Muslims, atheists, or agnostics?

5. Agree or disagree: If you are sure you are eternally secure no matter what, then you are more likely to fall into a sinful lifestyle than a person who believes he will go to hell if he falls away. Defend your answer.

6. Do you agree that people in most Christian traditions are not grateful to God specifically for eternal security? Why or why not?

7. What about people who believe that eternal security is true, but that no one can be sure if they are a "true believer" until they die? Many people who follow Reformed theology believe that. Is it

possible for such people to be grateful for eternal security? Why or why not?

8. Think of someone specific you know who is afraid of hell and who doesn't know where he is going when he dies. Do you believe this person would be better off or worse off if he came to be sure that simply by believing in Jesus he was eternally secure? Why?

CHAPTER 8: SEE LESS, ACCOMPLISH MORE

1. True or false: Sometimes you have to see less to accomplish more. Defend your answer.

2. How might fear of hell be a distraction that would keep you from focusing on eternal rewards?

3. Do you agree that a person who is sure they are eternally secure has a natural predisposition toward the idea of eternal rewards? Why or why not?

4. What is Lordship Salvation?

5. How might acceptance of the doctrine of eternal rewards set a person who held to Lordship Salvation free to be certain that all who simply believe in Jesus have eternal life?

6. Trace 2 Peter 1:5-11 and explain in your own words how the repetition of the verb "to add" or "to be supplied" illumines our understanding of the doctrine of rewards.

7. Why would misinterpreting rewards passages as kingdom entrance passages annihilate assurance? Pick one of the four passages used as illustrations to prove your point.

8. Is it selfish to strive for eternal rewards? Defend your answer.

CHAPTER 9: THE PROMISE OF EVANGELISM

1. Agree or disagree, and why: In the New Testament assurance is not a separate issue from the gospel because it is inherently contained in the gospel promises themselves.

2. Have you ever observed the approach which separates evangelism from assurance? That is the approach where first someone "leads a person to Christ" and only later talks about assurance of eternal life. If so, looking back on it, do you think it was a good or bad approach to use? Why?

3. Is it possible, in your opinion, to lead a person to faith in the Lord Jesus without mentioning what He promises the one who believes in Him? Why or why not?

4. Looking back on your own testimony, do you think you were born again before or at the moment you gained certainty you had eternal life? Explain.

5. Do you agree that it is tragic to fail to tell people about assurance when you are evangelizing? Why or why not?

6. Do you agree with the suggestion that there are three essentials which must always be brought up when we evangelize and that they are 1) Jesus, 2) eternal life, and 3) believing? Would you add any other essentials? Would you take away any of these?

7. Do most people grasp the idea of *eternal security* when they are told that Jesus *saves* those who believe in Him? Explain your answer.

8. If a person is a wonderful Christian but doesn't believe in eternal security, do they believe the gospel? Why or why not? And, if a person has *never* believed in eternal security, have they been born again? Why or why not? In light of your answers, do you think we should evangelize "Christians" who don't believe in eternal security?

CHAPTER 10: WILL THE REAL CHRISTIAN PLEASE STAND UP?

1. Define what a false professor is.

2. What is it that false professors believe about Jesus according to Lordship Salvation?

3. What is it that false professors believe about Jesus according to the author?

4. How do you distinguish a true professor from a false professor?

5. Explain how Matthew 7:21-23 relates to assurance.

6. Do you agree that unbelievers might pass various moral and attitudinal tests for true professors? Why or why not?

7. Do you agree that some believers might fail such tests? Why or why not?

8. Agree or Disagree? If a person believes in Jesus but also believes that in order to make it into the kingdom they must persevere in faith and good works, they are nonetheless born again. They are simply confused, and their confusion causes them to add in the requirements of works and of perseverance. Defend your answer.

CHAPTER 11: WHY NOT LIVE LIKE THE DEVIL?

1. Is believing that Jesus guarantees eternal life to all who simply believe in Him a bit like letting go of the branch? Why or why not?

2. Name some ways in which godliness is profitable in this life.

3. Do you know of any godly people who have experienced those benefits. Tell a bit about one such person.

4. Without naming names, tell about someone you've known who pursued a sinful lifestyle to their own detriment.

5. Name some ways in which godliness is profitable for the life to come.

6. Do you expect that all believers will have the same level of joy and abundance of life as all others? Or do you believe that some will have fuller lives than others? Defend your answer.

7. Do you want to rule with Christ in the life to come? Why or why not?

8. Agree or disagree: Godliness is the only sensible way to live. Defend your answer.

CHAPTER 12: CONTEMPLATING APPROVAL

1. What is the biblical purpose for self-examination?
2. What is it that you should examine when you practice spiritual self-examination?
3. How often should you practice spiritual self-examination?
4. Agree or disagree: Paul affirmed assurance apart from works.
5. Agree or disagree: Christians may or may not abide in the faith.
6. Discuss the use of the word *disqualified* in 1 Corinthians 9:27 and how it has bearing on 2 Corinthians 13:5-7.
7. Do you believe that Jesus approves of you today? Why or why not?
8. Do you desire Christ's approval at His Judgment Seat more than you desire the approval of anyone on earth? Why or why not?

CHAPTER 13: WHAT IF WE FAIL TO PERSEVERE?

1. Define perseverance.
2. Could a person believe perseverance is required to get into the kingdom and yet also be sure he was eternally secure?
3. Agree or disagree: Perseverance is not guaranteed.
4. Name some of the consequences in this life when a believer fails to persevere.
5. Name some of the consequences in the life to come for a believer who fails to persevere.
6. What motivates you to persevere in faith and good works?
7. If the rapture doesn't occur in our lifetime, how many more years do you think you are likely to live? Do you think it is going to be difficult to persevere for that long? Explain your answer.
8. Do you think that persevering in secular matters like pursuing your education, training for a marathon, training your children day by day, and the like makes it more likely that you will persevere in the Christian life? Why or why not?

CHAPTER 14: FRACTURED FAITH

1. Is it possible for born-again people to stop believing one of the fundamentals of the faith? Defend your answer.

2. Show from Ephesians 2:8-9 and other Scriptures that salvation, not faith, is the gift of God.

3. The idea that saving faith is a unique kind of faith is foreign to the Bible. Do you agree or disagree? Defend your answer.

4. Is it theoretically possible that God could ensure that no believer ever stopped believing in Christ? Why or why not?

5. Assume for the moment that God could ensure that believers never stop believing. Why wouldn't God do that if He could? What possible benefit could there be in allowing believers the possibility of such major failure?

6. If we are justified by faith in Christ and we stop believing in Him, why wouldn't that mean that we cease to be justified?

7. Do you believe that you might commit apostasy? Why or why not?

8. How do you guard against the possibility that you might commit apostasy?

CHAPTER 15: TESTING FIRST JOHN

1. What are the best arguments that the purpose of First John is assurance of eternal life? That is, what suggests John is giving a number of tests whereby a person can see if he's born again or not?

2. If assurance were dependent at least in part on our works, then could you ever be certain that you had eternal life? Why or why not?

3. If assurance was dependent at least in part on our sensitivity to sin, then could you ever be certain that you had eternal life? Why or why not?

4. Do you believe it's possible to be certain that you are *in fellowship* with God using the life tests that John gives? Why or why not?

5. Briefly explain what the four "these things I/we have written" verses in First John refer to. That is, which of these four is the purpose of the whole book and which of these are the purpose statements for paragraphs within the book?

6. Defend the view that 1 John 2:3-11 *is not* a discussion of how we know we are born again.

7. Defend the view that 1 John 2:3-11 *is* a discussion of how we know we are born again.

8. Compare 1 John 3:14 and John 5:24. Do you think it likely or unlikely that "passed from death into life" is used in precisely the same way in both passages? Defend your answer.

CHAPTER 16: CAMOUFLAGE CHRISTIANS

1. Have you ever failed to witness for Christ when you had an opportunity? If so, give an example.

2. What would you say are some good ways to motivate yourself to witness for Christ as much as is possible?

3. Do you think the fact that Jesus didn't *commit* Himself to the new believers of John 2:23-25 indicates that they didn't really believe in Him? Why or why not?

4. Look up the three references to Nicodemus in John's Gospel and discuss why you believe that each time John mentions that he came to Jesus by night.

5. Look at John 12:42-43 and the preceding context. Did many of the Jewish rulers actually believe in Jesus? Why or why not?

6. What did Jesus mean in Matthew 10:32-33 when He spoke of those whom He would confess and those whom He would deny?

7. Have you ever loved the praise of men more than the praise of God? Do you think that this is a temptation for every believer? Do you believe that none, some, most, or all believers succumb to this temptation during their lifetimes?

8.   If confessing our faith in Christ is required to get into the king-
     dom, then doesn't that mean that justification is not by faith
     alone? Why or why not?

CHAPTER 17: YOU WILL KNOW
THEM BY THEIR FRUITS

1.   Who are "they" in the expression "By their fruits you will know
     them" (Matthew 7:16, 20)?
2.   What are the fruits by which we identify "them"?
3.   Defend the view that the second soil in Luke 8:11-15 represents
     those who never truly believed in Jesus in the first place.
4.   Defend the view that the second soil in Luke 8:11-15 represents
     those who believed in Jesus and were born again, but who later
     fell away from the faith.
5.   Which of the soils do you believe represents, born-again people?
     Defend your answer.
6.   If a believer stops believing, then doesn't he become an unbeliever?
     Why or why not?
7.   Have you ever experienced spiritual distraction due to cares,
     riches, and pleasures of life? If so, explain.
8.   Agree or disagree: If fruit is required in order to know that you are
     born again, then certainty is impossible prior to death. Defend
     your answer.

CHAPTER 18: FACT OR FEELING?

1.   Do you think it is possible that your feelings might mislead you?
     Can you give an example from your life where following your
     feelings was (or would have been) a bad thing?
2.   Name some things you know are true based on how you feel (love,
     anger, discouragement, etc.).

3. Defend the view that Romans 8:16 is saying that the Holy Spirit produces some feeling within the believer that shows him that he is truly a child of God.

4. Give an example from the Gospels or Acts where someone was sure he was a child of God due to a feeling that the Holy Spirit produced within him.

5. Paul said, "We walk by faith, not by sight" (2 Corinthians 5:7). What bearing, if any, might that have to the question of feelings and assurance?

6. Agree or Disagree: If there really is some inner witness of the Holy Spirit and if that witness is necessary to have assurance, then certainty would be possible as long as the inner feeling were unmistakable. Defend your answer.

7. Agree or Disagree: If my feelings are at odds with the clear teaching of the Word of God, I should ignore my feelings and believe and do what the Bible says.

8. Agree or Disagree: There are times when I serve God that I actually do feel joy that I believe is from God and that confirms that I am a child of God. Why or why not?

CHAPTER 19: WHY IS CERTAINTY SO OBJECTIONABLE?

1. Agree or disagree: Eternal security apart from works makes it more likely that a person might indulge the flesh. That is, fear of hell makes a person less likely to choose a life of sin. Explain your answer.

2. Are you sure you have everlasting life no matter what? Why or why not?

3. If you are sure, then what motivates you to live for God when you don't have to in order to avoid hell?

4. What biblical evidence is there that fear of hell should motivate believers to live for God?

5. What biblical evidence is there that fear of hell should not motivate believers to live for God?

6. Certainty is not the historic position in Christianity and it isn't the majority position today either. Does that make it more or less likely that certainty is impossible prior to death? Why?

7. What role, if any, should tradition play in our understanding of Scripture?

8. Agree or disagree: God wants His children to be sure that they are eternally secure. Why or why not?

CHAPTER 20: ONLY GOD KNOWS

1. Compare Luke 18:9-14 with Luke 18:18-30. Do you think it likely that the point of the parable is related to the point of Jesus' encounter with the rich young ruler? Why or why not?

2. If you believe the parable and the rich young ruler passage are related, what would the parable suggest about how we should understand the rich young ruler passage?

3. Do you agree or disagree with the suggestion that believing in Jesus is bowing to His rule over your life? Why?

4. Do you agree or disagree with this statement: "Few today seem to understand the Bible's doctrine of assurance"? Defend your answer.

5. Is there one condition or multiple conditions in order to have eternal life? Defend your answer.

6. Is it true that the Westminster Confession of Faith raises questions that make certainty impossible prior to death? Defend your answer.

7. If only God knows who is saved, then how can anyone evangelize, knowing that he may actually be lost? Wouldn't it hinder a person from sharing the gospel if he himself wondered if he were even a child of God? Oppositely, wouldn't it improve one's evangelism to be sure? Defend your answer.

8. If only God knows who is saved, then how can anyone take comfort in the death of a believing loved one, as Paul says we should in 1 Thessalonians 4:18 (see verses 13-18), since it is quite possible that that loved one went to hell and not heaven?

CHAPTER 21: MANAGEABLE DISCOMFORT

1. Does it bother you that there are people training the next generation of pastors and missionaries who teach that we cannot be sure we have eternal life? Why or why not?

2. Why wouldn't someone want to put assurance in the category of percentages?

3. If assurance is always tinged with doubts, then what does "assurance" mean?

4. Agree or disagree? The more theological education a person has, the more likely it is that he isn't sure where he is going when he dies. Why or why not?

5. If you agreed with the previous statement, is it true that all Bible colleges and seminaries are equally likely to cause a person to lose his certainty? Why or why not?

6. If you believe in certainty, does that mean that you have a "preconceived system of theology" that keeps you from seeing the truth of Scripture that certainty is impossible? Why or why not?

7. Galatians 5:19-21 is parallel to 1 Corinthians 6:9-11. Read both passages. Do you see any sins in either list which you believe a born-again person might actually struggle with? (Hint: compare the list in Galatians 5:19-21 with 1 Corinthians 3:3.)

8. What does Dr. Belcher mean when he says that a believer should not "take his salvation for granted," nor "presume on the grace of God"? Do you agree or disagree with his concern here? Why?

CHAPTER 22: UNCERTAINTY IS BETTER THAN ANY OTHER OPTION

1. Does the presence of false professors in this world "cause genuine Christians to doubt their salvation?" Why or why not?

2. Do you think it is reasonable to be terrified, as Dr. Sproul testified he had been, if you have doubts about whether your destiny is heaven or hell? Explain your answer.

3. Dr. Sproul, unlike some other authors, suggests in his *TableTalk* article that our commitment and works cannot soothe our doubts. Which do you think is correct, that our commitment and works can or cannot soothe the doubts of a person who is unsure of his eternal destiny? Defend your answer.

4. What did Peter mean in John 6:68 when he said that Jesus had "words of eternal life"?

5. Was Peter certain or uncertain that he had eternal life? Defend your answer.

6. Is it wrong for a person to "flee to the cross to escape hell"? Why or why not?

7. Why does Dr. Sproul say that being uncomfortable with Jesus is better than any other option?

8. What do you make of the fact that, in books he wrote after his *TableTalk* article, Dr. Sproul implies that certainty is impossible, and yet also specifically says things like this: "It is of utmost importance that new Christians become *certain* of their personal salvation. Such assurance is a mighty boon to the growth of faith to maturity" (*Grace Unknown*, pp. 200-201, italics added)? On balance would you say, based on the quotes given, that he believes that one can or cannot be certain once and for all of his eternal destiny prior to death?

CHAPTER 23: A MYRIAD OF FACTORS TO CONSIDER

1. According to Dr. MacArthur, what is *cognitive assurance*?
2. What is *subjective assurance* according to Dr. MacArthur?
3. *Behavioral assurance*, according to Dr. MacArthur means what?
4. Do you think what Dr. MacArthur calls *behavioral assurance* is objective or subjective? Defend your answer.
5. Do you think it is possible that an unbeliever might be sensitive to sin? Why or why not?
6. Do unbelievers ever obey God's Word? Defend your answer.
7. Do unbelievers (e.g., Mormons, Jehovah's witnesses, Muslims) sometimes suffer rejection because of their faith? Defend your answer.
8. Do believers ever fail to see a decreasing pattern of sin in their lives? Do believers sometimes even see an *increasing* pattern of sin in their lives? Defend your answer.

Scripture Index

Matthew

4:4	144
6:19-21	63
7:14	160
7:15-16	138
7:15-20	139
7:16	138
7:20	138
7:21-23	82-84, 86, 139, 198
7:22	198
10:32	132-34
10:32-33	132
10:33	132-34
12:33	138
12:34	139
23:37	119

Luke

3:8	83
8:5	139
8:5-15	139
8:6-8	141
8:8	139
8:9-14	84
8:12	114-15, 139, 141
8:13	115, 139, 141-42
8:14	139, 142
8:15	139-140, 144
8:18	144
10:17	54
10:20	34, 53
15:11-24	109
18:9-14	47, 83, 85, 162
18:22	167

19:11-27 117
19:17 110

John

1:12 30
1:12-13 130
1:29 88
1:41-42 186
2 130-32
2:11 186
2:23 130
2:23-24 130
2:23-25 130-31
2:23-27 131
2:24 130
3 .... 132, 134
3:1 131
3:2 132
3:16 .... 25, 30, 75, 133, 162
3:16-18 186
3:18 ..... 25, 31, 89, 92, 185
3:36 .... 25, 31
4:10 .... 114, 119
4:10-14 85
4:14 31
5:24 .. 31, 75, 88-89, 92, 127, 185-86
6:28-29 87
6:34 18
6:35a 116
6:35 .... 18, 31, 116

6:35-40 .... 85, 185-86
6:38-49 87
6:47 ...... 15, 24, 31, 72, 75, 85, 131, 173, 186, 191, 198
7 132
7:17 119
7:50 132
8:21 92
8:24 .... 88, 92
8:31-32 47
10:9 31
10:10 97
10:10b 186
10:28 .... 31, 36
10:28-30 36
11 31-33
11:25 19
11:25-26 .... 31, 206
11:25-27 .. 19, 75, 84-85, 164
11:26 ...... 19-20, 88, 116, 185, 198
11:26b 32
11:27 20
12 134
12:42-43 132
12:43 135-36
12:50 31
13:10 31
14:6 186

14:21 131

15:3 102

15:4 102

15:15 131

16:9-11 122

19 . . . . 132, 134

19:39 132

20:31 . . . . 32-33, 85

Acts

10:44 119

10:47 34

15:7-11 25

16:14 . . . . 114, 119

16:31 26

17:6 202

17:11 14

Romans

3:20 162

3:24 114

4:5 26

7:13-25 47

8:15 150

8:16 150-51

8:17a 174

8:26 150

10:2 83

12 144

12:2 119

14:10-13 104

1 Corinthians

1:1 105

1:11 100

2:5 100

2:14 103

3:1 34

3:1-3 . . . . 84, 100

3:3 100

3:5 100

3:10-15 104

5:9–6:20 100

6 175

6:1-20 84

6:9-10 175

6:9-11 175

6:12-20 84

6:15 85

6:15-20 174

6:18-19 85

6:19 100-101

6:19-20 34

9:24-25 108

9:24-27 . . . . 66, 104

9:27 . . . . 69, 103, 105,
107-108, 190, 203

11:21 100

11:30 . . . . 84, 100

15:2 100

15:11 100

15:14 100

15:17 100

16:13 100-102

2 Corinthians

1:24 100

4:4 114

5:8 105

5:9-10 . . . . 68, 89, 104

5:10 92

5:14 46

5:14-15 61

10:15 100

11 60

13 172

13:5 . . . . 24, 99, 101,
104-105, 173

13:5-7 103

13:7 104

Galatians

1:6-9 82

2:4 82-83

2:15-16 . . . . 84-85, 162

2:16 . . . . 26, 174

2:20 67

3:1-5 82

3:6-7 26

3:6-14 162

5:1-15 82

5:13 48

5:15 47

5:19-21 104

5:26 48

6:7-9 104

Ephesians

1:13 27

2:5 . . . . 27, 34

2:7 202

2:8 34

2:8-9 . . . . 27, 114, 174

5:5-7 104

Philippians

1:21 105

3:11-14 104

4:3 . . . . 35, 105, 174

Colossians

1:21-23 104

2:7 101

1 Timothy

1:2 96

1:3-4 126

1:15-16 32

1:16 36

1:19 115

2:3-6 96

2:12 96

2:15 96

4:8 . . . . 93-94, 96, 158

6:6 96

6:14 96

6:19 96

2 Timothy

1:12 96

2:12 . . . . 66, 104, 107,
117, 134-35

2:12-13 134

2:13 116

2:15 . . . . 66, 69, 103-105

2:18 116

4:6-10 96

Titus

1:13 101

3:5 176

Hebrews

5:12 34

6:6 116

11 97

11:35 97-98

James

1:3 27

1:18 . . . . 27, 34

5:9 67

1 Peter

1:22-23 27

1:24-25 27

5:7 143

2 Peter

1:5-11 65

1:10-12 187

1 John

1:5-10 . . . . 125, 201

1:8 . . . . . . 122, 176, 189, 197

1:9 122-23

1:10 . . . . . 122, 176, 189, 197

1:11 176

2:1 125

2:2 88

2:3-11 126

2:22-23 123

2:24-25 125

2:25 32

2:26 125

2:28 68

3:2 118

3:14 127-128

3:16-18 . . . . 123, 203

4:17 68

4:17-19 68

4:19 61

5:9-12 125

5:9-13 . . . . 123, 128, 151

5:13 124-25

Revelation

2:7 110

2:17 110

2:26 107

3:4-5 . . . . 108, 110

20:5 19

20:11-13 92

20:11-15 86

20:15 92

22:14 110

22:17 . . . . 85, 114

Subject Index

abundant

eternal experience 97

life 109, 118, 158

apostate 114

approval 66, 99-100,
103-105, 108-10, 203

approved 66, 103-104

assurance 12-13, 17-18,
20, 23, 25, 29-30, 33-37,
40-42, 45-49, 55, 58, 60,
64, 67-68, 71, 73-74, 77,
91, 100-101, 105, 107-108,
110, 114, 118, 121-25,
127-31, 135, 137, 144-45,
147, 149, 151-52, 161-64,
166-67, 169-74, 177, 179,
182-83, 185-89, 193-96, 198

Belcher 169-80

belief 33, 72, 117, 141

believe ... 9-10, 13-15, 17-21,
24-26, 28, 30-33, 35-36,
39-42, 46-47, 49, 51, 55,
58-60, 64-65, 67-69, 71-77,
81-83, 85-92, 95, 98,
108, 110, 114-16, 119,
130-32, 134-36, 140-41,
145-46, 152, 155-56,
158-60, 163-67, 172-74,
178, 182-83, 185, 192,
194-95, 198-199, 202-203,
205-206

Bema 67-68

Calvinist 65, 156, 182

certainty 9-10, 12-14,
23-24, 26, 28, 32, 35,
41, 45-46, 59-60, 65,

73, 77, 98, 114,
118, 155-56, 158-60,
162, 164-66, 169-73,
176, 179, 182-85,
187-89, 191, 194-95,
197, 199-203, 205-206

Chantry 161-67

commitment . . . 24, 37, 39-40,
72, 158, 177-78, 182

discipline 66, 102-104,
107, 109, 136, 157, 160

disqualified 66, 99, 103,
107

doubt 18, 20, 24, 27,
50, 101, 105, 130, 137,
144, 156, 158, 164, 169,
171, 173-74, 178, 182-83,
187, 191

eternal life 10, 12, 14,
18-20, 25, 28, 31-32,
35-42, 45-46, 49-51, 56,
58-59, 64, 67-69, 71-73,
75-76, 81, 85, 87-92, 96, 98,
100, 105, 108-109, 111,
114-16, 118, 133, 135-36,
145, 147, 149, 151, 156-59,
162-64, 166-67, 173-79,
182, 185-86, 190-91, 199,
202-203, 205

eternal security 14, 19, 25,
55, 57-59, 64, 69, 74,
76, 101, 118, 136, 156

eternally secure 10, 12-14,
18, 20, 25, 30, 33, 36,
42, 46, 54-55, 59, 62,
64, 69, 75, 77, 85, 94,
103, 115-16, 118, 123,
135-36, 147, 155-58,
166, 171-72, 183, 186,
194, 201-202, 205

evangelism 38, 71-77,
158-59, 161-62, 202

evangelize 13, 71, 77,
91, 202

everlasting life 145

false professors 13, 81-83,
85-86, 91, 100, 105,
178, 182-83, 191

fear 10, 12, 50,
58-60, 63-64, 68-69,
103, 108, 118, 132,
156-57, 183-84, 187, 205

fears 171

feelings 13, 25, 28,
48-49, 149, 151-52,
172-73

fellowship . . . 38, 109, 122-26,
128, 170

flesh 48, 67, 73, 96,
117, 142, 194

forgiveness 176

fruit 13, 89-90, 110,
137-40, 142-43, 146,
190-91

gift 10, 27, 34, 85,
111, 114, 163

good news 12, 38, 60, 68,
72-75, 83, 85, 89, 136,
140, 152, 157, 202-203

grace 26-27, 34, 36,
46, 51, 59, 61, 65, 86,
111, 156, 165, 177, 187,
189, 192-93, 195, 202

gratitude 10, 13, 18,
20, 45-46, 50, 57-62,
64, 166, 179, 186

Great White Throne 86,
88, 92, 139

heaven 24, 34, 41, 47,
55-56, 69, 72-73, 81,
85-86, 91-92, 133-34,
152, 171, 179, 183

Hodges 174

holiness 84, 98, 126,
131, 156

insecurity 11, 50, 65, 69

jealousy 131

joy 13, 18, 53-55,
57, 59, 97-98, 109,
124-25, 136, 160,
188, 201

Judgment Seat 47, 67-68,
73, 100, 103-105,
134, 136

Justification 26, 38, 41,
47, 68, 82, 85, 87, 90,
101-102, 105, 145,
159-160, 165, 176

justifies 26

legalism 46-48, 59, 61,
82, 145

Lordship Salvation 64-65,
177

MacArthur 49, 193-99

Manageable Discomfort . . 169

mature . . . 45, 48, 50, 68, 122,
126, 139-40, 142, 146

motivation 10, 13, 60,
98, 131, 157, 185

obedience 13, 49-50, 66,
96, 98, 109, 122, 158,
164-65, 182, 184-85, 191

Paul 25-28, 35, 46-48,
50-51, 60-61, 66-67, 82-85,
94-105, 107-108, 115,
119, 131, 134, 144, 150,
172-76, 190

persecution 136

perseverance . . . 13, 32, 65-66,
69, 107-108, 110-11,
156, 158, 182, 189

pride 118

promise 38-39, 41-42,
49, 71-77, 105,
149, 152

Reformed . . 182-84, 187, 192

reign 66, 107, 135

renewing 144

resurrection 19-20, 31-33,
36, 75, 202-203, 206

rewards 13, 46-47, 51,
63-66, 68-69, 96, 103,
105, 110-11, 160

righteousness 26, 47, 51,
83, 176

root 89-90

salvation 12, 36, 39, 42,
74-75, 83, 101, 109,
114, 121, 123,
127-29, 135, 161-62,
182, 184, 187-90,
194-96, 199

sanctification 102, 105,
176, 187-88

saving faith 114-15, 158,
163, 182, 190

security 10, 23, 25, 206

shame 116

soul 46, 163, 187

Sproul 181-92

sure 10-14, 24, 26,
28, 35-37, 40-42, 45,
48, 50, 60, 64, 66,
69, 83, 91

uncertainty 10, 14, 46,
60, 159-60, 181,
186-87, 191

well done 47, 67,
103-104, 110,
144, 203

Word of God 14, 37, 77,
95, 102-105, 118-19,
122, 126, 144, 146,
149, 151-52, 160-61, 185

works 10, 18, 24-28,
34, 46-47, 50-51, 64,
69, 72, 82-88, 90-92,
97-98, 100-102, 104-105,
107-109, 111, 121,
137-41, 145-47, 156,
158, 160, 172-73, 177,
179, 184, 190-92

worry 108, 130, 137,
170, 174, 184

Annotated Bibliography

The following are what I believe to be the leading works on assurance in English. I've included theses, dissertations, and newsletter and journal articles on the subject.

Achmoody, Jason. "Jonathan Edwards' Doctrine of Perseverance as it Relates to the Nature of Saving Faith and Christian Assurance." Unpublished Th.M. Thesis (Department of Historical Theology), Dallas Theological Seminary, May 2002.

The author, who agrees with Edwards, concludes that "Perseverance is an essential part of justifying faith and though not the cause of our salvation remains nevertheless a condition of it" (p. 64). "Perseverance is virtually a part of saving faith" (p. 65). Assurance based on simply believing the promise of the good news, he suggests, is rightly called "a sop for spiritual indifference" (p. 65). I highly recommend this work for it shows the position of extreme Calvinism.

Barker, Harold. *Secure Forever*. Neptune, NJ: Loizeaux Brothers, 1974. 190 pages.

Though this book is principally about eternal security, it does discuss assurance as certainty (see pp. 32-33, "A Sure Knowledge"; see also pp. 20-22, "Eternal Life—Our Present Possession"). While I wish there was more on assurance, what is in this book is helpful. I recommend it.

Beeke, Joel R. *The Quest for Full Assurance: The Legacy of Calvin and His Successors.* Grand Rapids: The Banner of Truth Trust, 1999. 395 pages.

This book is a simplified version of his 1988 dissertation. It is easy to follow. "Full assurance," we discover, is not certainty, but a high level of probability one is born again. In his conclusion he states, "Assurance involves objective promises, subjective sanctification, and internal testimony" (p. 283). A bit later he adds, "Assurance grows by faith in the promises of God, by inward evidences of grace, and by the witness of the Spirit. Each of these types of assurance should be diligently prayed for and pursued; none should be separated from the others for undue emphasis on one will lead to a distortion of others" (p. 285). I highly recommend this work, though I disagree with its conclusions.

Bell, M. Charles. *Calvin and Scottish Theology: The Doctrine of Assurance.* Edinburgh: The Handsel Press, 1985. 211 pages.

Bell shows that the problems he discusses historically in Scottish Calvinism still plague the church today. He shows how Scottish Calvinism departed from Calvin and Campbell. One of the more fascinating observations he makes several times is that this type of Calvinism leads many to abstain from partaking of the Lord's Supper for fear that since they cannot be sure that they are elect, they might incur the judgment of God by partaking in an unworthy manner (see, for example, pp. 7-8, 201-202). I recommend Bell's work.

Boice, James Montgomery. *Christ's Call to Discipleship.* Chicago: Moody Press, 1986. 169 pages.

While not on assurance, there are several chapters (4, 8, 9, 14) directly related to assurance. Note this statement, "Jesus was strong on cautioning against presumption. He let no one think that he could presume to be a Christian while at the same time disregarding or disobeying His teachings…If we are not listening to Christ and are not following Him in faithful obedience, we are not his" (p. 166).

Borchert, Gerald L. *Assurance and Warning.* Nashville: Broadman Press, 1987. 214 pages.

The cover of the book has this statement: "[This book discusses] the balance between assurance and warning in 1 Corinthians, John, and

Hebrews." And what is that balance? Here Borchert is not very clear. He suggests that there is a tension: "They [genuine people of God] can live with the tension of assurance and warning" (p. 214, italics his). He then makes this fascinating comment in the last sentence of the entire book: "They can live with this tension because in Christ they know they will persevere to the end!" (p. 214). But how to do they know this if the warnings are genuine warnings, which Borchert says they are? The answer is, no one can be sure he will persevere to the end and if that is required to have assurance, then no one can have assurance until he has died. I recommend this highly.

Chafer, Lewis Sperry. _Systematic Theology_. 8 Vols. Dallas: Dallas Seminary Press, 1948.

There is much in these volumes on assurance. See especially Volume 3, on the doctrine of salvation, and Volume 7, containing his doctrinal summarizations. Note this summary statement concerning 1 John 5:12-13: "Thus God has revealed it is the divine purpose that everyone who believes to the saving of his soul may _know_ that he is saved, not in this instance through uncertain Christian experience but on the ground of that which is written in Scripture...The Word of God thus becomes a title deed to eternal life, and it should be treated as an article of surety, for God cannot fail in any word He has spoken" (Volume 7, p. 24, italics his).

Chantry, Walter. _Today's Gospel: Authentic or Synthetic?_ Carlisle, PA: The Banner of Truth Trust, 1970. 94 pages.

While not on assurance, the small book is related to assurance. His view is that only God knows who is truly born again. See especially Chapter 5, "Preaching Assurance and Acceptance with God," pp. 67-77. I discuss Chantry's view of assurance and give excerpts from _Today's Gospel_ in Chapter 20 of _Secure and Sure_.

Cole, Donald. _How to Know You're Saved_. Chicago: Moody Press, 1988. 63 pages.

Cole says "assurance is certainty" (p. 54). This is great. However, most of this book is not on certainty, but on "The Basis of Salvation" (Chapter 1), and "The Way of Salvation" (Chapter 2). Even the third and final chapter, "The Question of Sin" doesn't address assurance directly (though see p. 57 which suggests that certainty is found in understanding and believing God's Word). The appendix gives a clue to the author's purpose. There he deals with a number of problem texts concerning eternal security. Evidently this booklet is designed to prove eternal security.

There is some helpful material here. Unfortunately, Cole says one must not only believe in Jesus but also repent of his sins (pp. 21-22, 57). And he defines belief as more than "agree[ing] that certain things about Jesus are true" but as "belief that results in action, such as confessing Jesus as Lord. The one is intellectual assent; the other is genuine faith" (pp. 22-23).

Dillow, Joseph C. *The Reign of the Servant Kings: A Study of Eternal Security and the Final Significance of Man.* Hayesville, NC: Schoettle Publishing Co., 1992. 649 pages.

Dillow has two chapters dealing with assurance: Chapter 12, "Faith and Assurance" (pp. 271-91), and Chapter 13, "Self-Examination and Assurance" (pp. 293-310). Also related is his chapter entitled, "The Carnal Christian" (Chapter 14, pp. 311-31). This comment summarizes his basic view: "The Calvinist can offer no real assurance. A man has no assurance he is saved unless he is in a state of godly living at every moment. He therefore does not derive his comfort from Jesus' death; he derives his real comfort and assurance from his own works. Jesus may have saved him, but he can have no real assurance unless he has good works to show that He has really saved him. However, nothing more than looking to Christ is required, insofar as assurance of heaven is concerned" (pp. 308-309)." I highly recommend this book.

Eaton, Michael. *No Condemnation: A New Theology of Assurance.* Downers Grove, IL: InterVarsity Press, 1995. 261 pages.

Eaton shows that both Reformed (pp. 15-25) and Arminian theology (pp. 26-30) deny the possibility of certainty prior to death. Note this excellent statement concerning the Reformed view of assurance: "I have already urged that introspection is implicit in many aspects of the Reformed doctrine of grace in late Calvinism. Now I wish to underline the fact that the most intense introspection follows if many or all of these emphases are combined. If Christ did not die for all, and if it is possible to have a sorrow for sin which is not true repentance, a faith which is not true faith, a possessing of the Spirit which falls short of true regeneration, if despite any and every 'experience' of the gospel there is 'a way to Hell even from the Gate of Heaven', if

Paul himself feared loss of salvation, then what remains of the Calvinist's assurance? It has died the death of a thousand qualifications. No wonder a great Calvinist evangelist [Nettleton] could say, 'The most that I have ventured to say respecting myself is, that I think it possible I may get to heaven'" (p. 23). Some of the other topics discussed by Eaton are the role of hermeneutics in assurance, universal atonement, the Law of Moses, justification, motivation to live for God for people who are certain of their eternal security, and New Testament warnings. This book is highly recommended.

Gerstner, John H. *The ABC's of Assurance*. Ligonier, PA: Soli Deo Gloria Publications, 1991. 112 pages.

At the outset Gerstner states, "It is a duty *to be sure* [of eternal salvation]" (p. ii, emphasis added). A few pages later he adds, "Temporary assurance is no assurance at all" (p. 2). Yet he quickly turns around and implies that certainty is impossible when he asks whether in 1 Corinthians 9:26-27 Paul was "admitting that he could be lost?" (p. 5). His answer seems to be yes: "[Paul] said only that if he did [become the slave of his body], he would be rejected by God." He then concludes, "Every Christian must say the same thing. If he gives himself over to lust or lying or any other sin, he will be damned because he thereby proves himself not to be a Christian" (p. 6, emphasis his). Later he chastises Dispensationalists for suggesting that "once a person professes faith in Jesus Christ, he is going to be in Jesus Christ forever. He will never, no matter how he lives, cease to be saved in Christ" (p. 78). Gerstner does not suggest that the content of the professed faith is defective. Rather, he suggest that the test of saving faith is whether it is followed by good works. Though I am not in agreement with the late Dr. Gerstner, I strongly recommend this book.

Guinness, Os. *God in the Dark: The Assurance of Faith Beyond a Shadow of Doubt*. Wheaton, IL: Crossway Books, 1996. 224 pages.

Guinness argues that doubt and faith are not mutually exclusive. He manages this by having a view of unbelief that is novel: "The word unbelief is usually used [in the Bible] of a willful refusal to believe or a deliberate decision to disobey" (p. 26).

While he doesn't specifically define faith, by implication it is a willful decision to believe and a deliberate decision to obey.

What this book is really about is doubt. The chapter titles make this crystal clear. Every single chapter has the word doubt in the title or subtitle.

This book illustrates a major problem in Reformed thought. It produces rather than allays doubts. Guiness says, "over-sensitive [Calvinists] fasten on theological truths as on an armory of big sticks, and they rain down blows on their long-suffering faith, belaboring it for being substandard and for failing to believe what it should" (p. 34). In my experience nearly all 5-point Calvinists have doubts. The problem is their theological system, not their over-sensitivity.

Though discouraging, I highly recommend this book.

Heriot, M. Jean. *Blessed Assurance: Beliefs, Actions, and the Experience of Salvation in a Carolina Baptist Church.* **Knoxville, TN: The University of Tennessee Press, 1994. 255 pages.**

In this book the author examines how one church handled the question of assurance. She examined this church and found that it had great concerns about spurious believers. Thus they evaluated one's claim of faith in Jesus by his works. Blessed assurance was only available for the holy. Since the pastors of this church promoted a soft form of Lordship Salvation (see, for example, pp. 116-17), certainty was impossible for anyone following their teachings. This is a fascinating sociological study.

Hodges, Zane C. *Absolutely Free! A Biblical Reply to Lordship Salvation.* **Dallas and Grand Rapids: Redención Viva and Zondervan Publishing House, 1989. 238 pages.**

While this book isn't specifically about assurance, Hodges does cover the subject well (see pp. 49-52; see also pp. 94-95). I highly recommend this work.

_____. **"Assurance: Of the Essence of Saving Faith,"** *Journal of the Grace Evangelical Society* **(Spring 1997): pp. 3-17.**

Hodges argues that Calvin taught—and that the Bible teaches—that as long as one believes the good news he is sure he is eternally secure. This article can be read online at www.faithalone.org. It is outstanding and I highly recommend it.

_____. *The Gospel Under Siege: Faith and Works in Tension.* **Revised and Enlarged Edition. Dallas: Redención Viva, 1981, 1992. 184 pages.**

This book has a chapter on assurance (pp. 9-19). It also has a chapter in which Hodges shows that the tests of life view of First John doesn't fit the particulars of the letter (pp. 51-72). I highly recommend this book.

Ironside, H. A. *Full Assurance: How to Know You're Saved.* **Revised Edition. Chicago: Moody Press, 1968. 128 pages.**

Ironside takes a view on assurance that is somewhere between my view and that of authors like Lawson, MacArthur, and Whitney. Ironside repeatedly points people to the promises of God for assurance. This is excellent. Unfortunately, he instructs the reader to see if the world is less attractive to him (p. 85). If so, this should provide some level of assurance. Note how his view on First John is a sort of middle ground: "After emphasizing *these internal evidences of the new birth* so clearly in the early part of his letter [First John], the apostle [John] comes back in the closing portions to the great outstanding truth that *the surest proof of all is simple faith* in the testimony of God" (p. 85, italics added). When he discusses "Hindrances to Full Assurance" (pp. 89-125), he emphasizes repeatedly that it is simply faith in Christ that gives us assurance. Yet, he does say that one key to assurance is whether you "yield yourself to Him" (p. 90). Ironside ministered and wrote in a different era when these issues were not as sharply defined as they are today. Were he alive today, I believe he would agree with me. (Of course I do!) I recommend you get and read this book and decide for yourself.

Johnson, William Randall. "The Problem of Doubt in Philippians 3:11." Unpublished Master's Thesis (Department of New Testament Studies), Dallas Theological Seminary, May 1979.

I came across this thesis while a student at DTS. In it Johnson struggles with this text in light of his Reformed soteriology. He honestly admits it is hard for him to conclude that the apostle to the Gentiles was admitting in Philippians 3:11 that he was unsure he was regenerate. However, that is exactly what he concludes. This thesis is well worth reading.

Kendall, R. T. *Once Saved, Always Saved.* **Chicago: Moody Press, 1983. 238 pages.**

While this book is a defense of eternal security, it does discuss assurance. Kendall denies that assurance is tied to perseverance or good works (p. 21). Concerning the role of assurance in sanctification, he says: "It is only when the matter of assurance of eternal salvation is, as it were, completely behind you that you are truly ready to move on in the Christian life" (p. 59). "As long as there is doubt about your eternal standing in God's grace, there will be an impediment to your having fellowship with the Father" (p. 74). However, on the question of assurance being of the essence of saving faith, Kendall says no (pp. 110-12). I recommend this work.

Law, Robert. *The Tests of Life: A Study of the First Epistle of St. John.* **Edinburgh: T & T Clark, 1909. 422 pages.**

The classic text advocating First John as giving a series of tests to see if one is truly born again or not.

Lawson, Steven. *Absolutely Sure: Settle the Question of Eternal Life.* **Sisters, OR: Multnomah Publishers, 1999. 190 pages.**

I love the title and subtitle. Unfortunately, the book doesn't deliver what the title and subtitle promise. Lawson begins by suggesting that simply by believing in Jesus one can be sure he is eternally secure (see pp. 23-24 under "How firm a foundation"). But then he defines saving faith this way: "Saving faith is the abandonment of my life to Christ who died for me. It is a decisive turning from sin and trusting Him to save me. More than mere intellectual assent and emotional feelings, it is a choice of my will to receive Christ to be my personal Lord and Savior" (p. 25). Later he adds, "I can know that I have truly believed in Christ as I see His life-changing power in my life…This is not a works salvation, but a salvation that works" (p. 31). Most of the remainder of the book examines nine "vital signs" which he finds in First John (pp. 33, 47-170). This book is well written and easy to follow.

Lutzer, Erwin W. *How You Can Be Sure That You Will Spend Eternity with God.* **Chicago: Moody Press, 1996. 159 pages.**

This is another book, like Ironside's, that is very close to my position yet is somewhere in between my position and that of authors like

Larson, MacArthur, and Whitney. Lutzer points to faith in the promises of God as the sole basis of assurance. And there is no discussion in this book of First John and tests of life! That in itself is quite telling. I'd say Lutzer is essentially advocating my view, though there are a few statements that are fuzzy since he feels that if saving faith doesn't produce clear transformation in a person's life, then he has reason to doubt his standing with God. For example, he says that if a person told him "that he has accepted Christ as his Savior and yet lives the same selfish, sin-oriented life as before, I have reason to think that he might just be self deceived. After all, as this book has shown, the work of God in the heart is deep and lasting. Not only should we question someone's salvation if his life is unchanged, but he should question it too" (p. 118). I see this as an inconsistency in his position, rather than a central tenet. In any case, I recommend this book.

MacArthur, John F., Jr., *Saved Without a Doubt: How to Be Sure of Your Salvation*. Wheaton: Victor Books, 1992. 187 pages.

As with Lawson's book (see above), I love the title and subtitle. And again, this book doesn't deliver what the title and subtitle promise. Instead of Lawson's nine "vital signs" in First John, MacArthur finds eleven tests of his own (pp. 67-91, "Eleven Tests from an Apostolic Expert"). These eleven tests are designed to show someone whether he is truly saved. Unfortunately, since all eleven tests are subjective, it would be impossible for anyone following his tests to be sure. While this book is well worth having and reading, I believe that Lawson has done a better job of presenting the same view in a way that is easy to follow.

MacDonald, William. *Once in Christ, in Christ Forever: More Than 100 Biblical Reasons Why a True Believer Cannot Be Lost*. Grand Rapids: Gospel Folio Press, 1997. 208 pages.

Here's another book on eternal security that briefly touches on assurance. Chapter 11 is entitled, "Assurance or Uncertainty" (pp. 47-49). There he says, "It's no wonder that God's people down through the centuries have rested their assurance of heaven on the work of Christ alone and not on any unpredictable and dubious achievements of their own...The moment you add legal conditions to be fulfilled by the believer, assurance is impossible, because you can't know if he or she will fulfill the conditions properly" (p. 49). This is terrific. However, in the next two chapters he hedges his position saying that true believers will not apostatize (see pp. 69-70) and that Old Testament people mentioned by Jude "were never born again" and the proof he cites is their "lives," not their lack of faith in Jesus (p. 77; see also p. 129). MacDonald takes the tests of life view of First John (pp. 91-96, 125-29). This book straddles the fence, suggesting that only faith is needed for assurance, but that if the life doesn't match up, the person proves he really isn't born again. While I appreciate the defense of eternal security, the material on assurance is confusing.

Marshall, I. Howard. *Kept by the Power of God: A Study of Perseverance and Falling Away*. London: Epworth Press, 1969. 228 pages.

The author believes that eternal life can be lost by failing to persevere. Thus Marshall feels it is impossible prior to death to be sure where you will spend eternity since failing to persevere means you will end up in hell and persevering means you will make it into the kingdom.

Minirth, Frank B. "The Pychological Effects of Lordship Salvation," *Journal of the Grace Evangelical Society* (Autumn 1993): pp. 39-51.

While this article—by a leading Christian psychiatrist—isn't on assurance per se, it is all about assurance. Lordship Salvation "makes assurance *conditional* and the best anyone can hope for is to have enough good works to be *somewhat* confident of salvation" (p. 39). I highly recommend this article, available at www.faithalone.org.

Moyer, R. Larry. *Free and Clear: Understanding & Communicating God's Offer of Eternal Life*. Grand Rapids: Kregel Publications, 1997. 272 pages.

This book on evangelism contains a fairly long chapter on assurance (pp. 57-84). Moyer feels that assurance is not of the essence of saving faith (p. 54). Rather, he feels "it is virtually impossible for new believers to make strides spiritually if they don't have the matter of their eternal destiny settled" (p. 54). The author asserts that our works are not the basis of assurance (p. 55)! Instead, he says that assurance is based on faith alone (pp. 58-61). "A person who wants to know if he or she is a Christian has only to answer one question: Am I trusting Christ alone for my eternal salvation?" (p. 79). Moyer also has a nice discussion of the parable of the four soils (pp. 62-63), 2 Corinthians

13:5 (pp. 66-67), James 2:14-26 (pp. 72-77), and other potential problem texts as well. I recommend this book.

Nichols, Stephen. *An Absolute Sort of Certainty: The Holy Spirit and the Apologetics of Jonathan Edwards.* **Phillipsburg, NJ: P & R Publishing, 2003. 202 pages.**

While this book is about certainty that God's Word is true, not about one's personal regeneration, Nichols does spend two chapters (Chapters 4 and 5, pp. 77-153) talking about what Edwards believed about assurance of eternal life. Unfortunately, Nichols *tells us* what Edwards believed as often as he *shows us* from his writings. Nichols suggests that Edwards taught that assurance can and should be more than probability (pp. 102-104). Yet he also shows where Edwards taught that one must look at his works to see if he is a true or false professor (pp. 116-21). This seems to contradict the suggestion that certainty is possible. Note this statement by Nichols: "[Edwards] argues that the more one obeys the demands of the gospel [!], and the longer one lives a life of obedience, the greater one's sense of assurance will be" (pp. 117-18). If this is true, then one would never be sure until death, for one can always grow in his life of obedience, and future defection is always possible as well.

Pak, Joseph K. "A Study of Selected Passages on Distinguishing Marks of Genuine and False Believers." Unpublished Ph.D. Dissertation (Department of New Testament Studies), Dallas Theological Seminary, May 2001. 331 pages.

According to this doctoral thesis, "There are striking similarities between false believers and genuine believers (chapter 3). False believers accept the gospel truth, [and] make profession [sic] of faith in Jesus so that they are accepted into the believing community as its members. They may even have many of the same spiritual experiences that genuine believers have as members of the same community" (p. 297). How then does one have assurance that he is a genuine believer? This is where "distinguishing marks" come into play. There are three. "First, the indwelling Holy Spirit in genuine believers provides them subjective element [sic] of assurance in addition to the objective testimony of Scripture. Second, actions consistent with the profession of faith mark genuine believers...Third, genuine believers do not finally reject their faith. They may fall into doubts on occasion, but God's sovereign grace does not let them abandon their faith altogether. This mark also serves as a warning to false believers not to turn away from the Christian faith they profess" (p. 298). I highly recommend this work for it shows that for many today assurance is far from certainty. If false believers actually do "accept the gospel truth" and if they "may even have many of the same spiritual experiences that genuine believers have as members of the same community," then prior to death no one can be sure whether he is a genuine believer or a false professor.

Schreiner, Thomas R. and Ardel B. Caneday. *The Race Set Before Us: A Biblical Theology of Perseverance & Assurance.* **Downers Grove, IL: InterVarsity Press, 2001. 344 pages.**

This work is similar to Borchert (see above) and Volf (see below). The authors argue that there is a tension between the warnings and promises of Scripture. They repeatedly speak of salvation as being already-but-not-yet. However, the already aspect often gets swallowed up and what is left is *maybe not.* Consider this statement: "We must run the race with dogged determination to obtain the prize of eternal life, and it takes remarkable discipline and training to make it to the end...Saying that we must run the race to the end can scarcely be called works-righteousness, since such persevering faith is ultimately the gift of God!" (p. 314). I recommend this book.

Sproul, R. C. *Grace Unknown: The Heart of Reformed Theology.* **Grand Rapids: Baker Books, 1997. 230 pages.**

Here is another work that merely touches on assurance. Even so, it is well worth reading. Assurance is discussed on pp. 199-209. Sproul suggests that progress and perseverance in good works indispensable to assurance. See Chapter 22 in *Secure and Sure* for excerpts from this book.

_____. **"Assurance of Salvation,"** *TableTalk* **(November 1989): p. 20.**

This is an amazing account of one man's struggle with personal assurance.

Stanley, Charles. *Eternal Security: Can You Be Sure?* Nashville: Oliver Nelson, 1990. 194 pages.

This book is primarily a defense of eternal security. Only secondarily does it deal with the issue of assurance. Even so, this book is helpful on assurance. Stanley holds precisely the same view of assurance as reflected in *Secure and Sure*. I highly recommend this book.

Steele, David N., Curtis C. Thomas, and Lance S. Quinn. *The Five Points of Calvinism: Defined, Defended, and Documented.* Second Edition. Phillipsburg, NJ: P & R Publishing, 2004. 248 pages.

The classic explanation of five-point Calvinism was originally published in 1963. Forty years later, and over a decade after Steele's death, Thomas, with the help of Quinn, revised and expanded this classic. Assurance only receives passing attention in this book. Still it is well worth reading the concerns the authors express about too much introspection. Note this warning: "Another odd pitfall that characterizes some Calvinists is chronic introspection. Now, I do not mean normal self-examination (2 Cor. 13:5). I mean the sort that goes too far. This sort seems to glory in introspection without the proper results. What do I mean? True self-examination should lead to more faith and love and obedience. False introspection leads to more introspection, and actually less faith. It produces more doubt, not faith. For example, some worry that they might not be among the elect. But this does not lead them to put faith in Christ. If that is the result, then it is not true self-examination...Be careful" (p. 195). How one gets the desired result out of self-examination is not stated. Certainly merely desiring the right result doesn't produce it or else this wouldn't be a problem for "some Calvinists." I commend Thomas and Quinn for pointing out this problem. I highly recommend this book.

Strombeck, J. F. *Shall Never Perish*. Moline, IL: Strombeck Agency, 1936. 195 pages.

This book is a solid defense of eternal security. Unfortunately, there isn't much here on assurance that one is eternally secure. (See pages 1-5 for his discussion of assurance.)

Volf, Judith Gundry. *Paul and Perseverance: Staying In and Falling Away.* **Louisville, KY: Westminster/John Knox Press, 1990. 325 pages.**

This is a very scholarly treatment of the subject. While not on assurance per se, the entire book discusses the issue. Her conclusion is that Christians do not know, in this life, their eternal destiny: "Subjection to antagonistic forces at work in such tribulation can even threaten their salvation. Moreover, they have yet to appear before the judgment seat at which occasion their final destiny will be made manifest. Will they be accused and condemned after all?" (p. 283). Volf views the Judgment Seat of Christ as the same judgment as the Great White Throne Judgment. In this one final judgment people will only then learn their eternal destiny. I highly recommend this work.

Whitney, Donald S. *How Can I Be Sure I'm a Christian? What the Bible Says About Assurance of Salvation.* **Colorado Springs: NavPress, 1994. 153 pages.**

Like Lawson and MacArthur, Whitney fails to deliver what his title promises. He splits the difference between Lawson's nine tests and MacArthur's eleven. He finds ten tests of true faith (pp. 52-64). Since his tests are subjective as well, if one follows his tests, he cannot be sure prior to death. One difference with this book is that at the end of the book, after dealing with false assurance and the ten tests, he has a final chapter entitled, "What to Do if You Are Still Not Sure" (pp. 135-53). It is truly fascinating and worth the price of the book all by itself.

Wilkin, Robert N. *An Exegetical Evaluation of the Reformed Doctrine of the Perseverance of the Saints.* **Unpublished Master's Thesis, Dallas Theological Seminary, 1982.**

I argue that eternal security is true whether a believer perseveres or not. Perseverance is commanded, but not guaranteed. It is a mistake to link our assurance with our perseverance.

_____. **"Saints: Spurious or Secret,"** *Grace in Focus* **(November–December 1996).**

Here I discuss the idea of false professors as they relate to secret believers in John's Gospel. Available at www.faithalone.org.

Testimonials

The following are portions of testimonies from men and women from around the United States who have been tremendously impacted by the certain knowledge of their eternal life. Their full testimonies can be found at www.faithalone.org.

Jay Bockisch
Engineer

In Seattle I met two Christians who had tremendous hearts for Jewish people. They became friends and challenged me with the gospel. As time went on I could not stop thinking about Jesus. I began to study the Old and New Testaments and other books. After reading several books on Messianic prophecy, I accepted Jesus as the Messiah and Savior.

Lauren Bockisch
Homemaker

After intensive study on the subject of assurance, I was overjoyed to know for certain that I have everlasting life. Jesus said, "He who believes in Me has everlasting life" (John 6:47). I learned that the reason He could fulfill such a wonderful promise is because when He died on the cross, "the Lord laid on Him the iniquity of us all" (Isaiah 53:6). When I believed in Him for eternal life, I entered into an incredibly beautiful and eternal relationship with the Lord. Since that time I have continued to be sure I am an eternally secure child of God.

Diane Boring
Homemaker

I have never stopped believing Jesus' promise of eternal life since I came to faith in High School. No matter what trials have come into my life, I've always known I'm saved for eternity based upon the sure promise of God recorded in His Word—that whoever believes in Him shall not perish but have everlasting life. That assurance has brought me peace for more than 40 years now. It's the only way to live!

Paul Carpenter
Pastor

Today, I serve in liberty from the tyranny of fear that I knew for so many years. As for me, I am adamantly opposed to the doctrine of assurance by works. Only by beginning with assurance based solely on the promise of God is the believer free to go on to maturity. Looking at our imperfect works will never lead to assurance. An inward focus for assurance makes spiritual maturity utterly impossible.

Leslie Jensen
Accountant Turned Homemaker

It wasn't until our family started attending a church in Southern California that I got it. I learned that my own works do not impact God's promise of eternal life to me, whether the works happen before or after I believe in His Son. I am fully and finally secure on the basis of God's promise alone. As I began to understand that, I came to realize just how much God loved me and how gracious He truly is.

Letitia Lii
Doctor of Optometry

I came to believe in Jesus Christ for eternal life one Easter Sunday. Although I felt so undeserving of Christ's sacrifice to pay for the penalty of my sins, I was just so thrilled to have eternal life.

Mike Lii
Entrepreneur

After Friday night service, a counselor finally explained the gospel to me. To have eternal life, one simply believed in Jesus for it with no works needed. I remember thinking "This is great and very important news! Why had no one else told me this before?" That night I believed in Jesus Christ for the free gift of eternal life.

Marialis Lopez
Financial Analyst

The best part of understanding God's message of grace is that I have assurance of my salvation. I have a different view of life now. I'm 100 percent sure that I will go to heaven when I die—not because of anything I've done, but all because of what Jesus did. Thank God for His grace and assurance!

René Lopez
Pastor/Doctoral Student

Until I realized that 100 percent certainty came at the very moment I believed in Christ, I was not saved and had no peace. If only someone had told me long ago that I could obtain assurance by having faith alone in Christ alone, perhaps I would not have made numerous mistakes. Learning the true gospel according John 6:47 at age 27 brought me certainty.

Stan Nelson
Retired John Deere Factory Worker

Understanding that salvation is "by grace through faith plus nothing" has removed any reason for despair or pride. All honor and glory go to Christ the Savior for doing the saving and the keeping.

Brian Stone
Chaplain

I was a person who was easy to hate and a person no one expected anything from. But the promises of God are so trustworthy that even I can and do have confidence in Christ.

Yami Valdez
Med Tech/Personal Trainer

A pastor showed me from the Bible that all who believe in Jesus are secure forever. Jesus said, "He who hears My word and believes in Him who sent Me has everlasting life, and shall not come into judgment, but has passed from death into life" (John 5:24). For the first time in my life, my fears were gone. I knew I had eternal life and could never lose it, not because I was good, but because Jesus guarantees eternal life to all who believe in Him.

A Word about Grace Evangelical Society

Grace Evangelical Society (GES) was founded in 1986 by Dr. Bob Wilkin as an educational and motivational networking ministry. The purpose of GES is to promote the clear proclamation of God's free salvation and related, yet distinct, discipleship issues. GES accomplishes this purpose by the following means:

- a free bimonthly newsletter,
- a semiannual journal,
- commentaries on New Testament books,
- books by authors such as Zane Hodges, Earl Radmacher, Jody Dillow, and Bob Wilkin,
- audio tapes,
- conferences and seminars, and
- a non-resident school of theology.

If you'd like to schedule Bob to speak at your church or conference, receive our free newsletter, or obtain more information about our various ministries and publications, you can contact us in any of the following ways:

972.257.1160 (phone),
972.255.3884 (fax),
ges@faithalone.org (email),
www.faithalone.org (website), or
PO Box 155018, Irving, TX 75015-5018.

If you enjoyed *Secure and Sure* may we suggest...

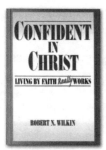

Confident in Christ: Living by Faith Really Works (287 pages)
Do you have questions as to what the Bible says about salvation? This book will help you understand and proclaim the gospel with clarity and precision. *Confident in Christ* has been used by pastors and lay people alike to clarify gospel issues.

The Road to Reward: Living Today in Light of Tomorrow (197 pages)
What will eternity be like? How will the manner in which we live today affect our lives in the coming kingdom? Bob answers these and many more questions in *The Road to Reward*.

When most Christians think about eternity, they envision floating on white clouds, strumming harps. One cannot help but wonder what we will do with all this time on our hands. If you have ever wondered what eternity will be like and how knowing this can change our lives here and now, *The Road to Reward* has been written with you in mind.

You Can Be Sure! (32 pages)
If you enjoyed *Secure and Sure*, you will find Dr. Wilkin's booklet on assurance to be an excellent and inexpensive way to share assurance with friends and loved ones. With over 100,000 in print, this is an extremely popular tool for evangelism and discipleship. (Spanish version: *¡Puedes Estar Seguro!*)

To order, call 972.257.1160 or visit us online at www.faithalone.org.